THE
LEGISLATIVE
COMMITTEE
GAME

THE LEGISLATIVE COMMITTEE GAME

A Comparative Analysis of Fifty States

Wayne L. Francis

Ohio State University Press
Columbus

Library of Congress Cataloging-in-Publication Data
Francis, Wayne L.
  The legislative committee game : a comparative analysis of fifty states / Wayne L. Francis.
    p. cm.
  Bibliography: p.
  Includes index.
  ISBN 0-8142-0484-8 (alk. paper)
  1. Legislative bodies—United States—States—Committees.
I. Title.
JK2495.F73   1989
328.73′0765—dc19   89-2899
                                                                                    CIP

The paper in this book meets the guidelines for permanence and durability of the Committee on Production Guidelines for Book Longevity of the Council on Library Resources.

Printed in the U.S.A.

9 8 7 6 5 4 3 2 1

13/001x

Contents

List of Illustrations   vii

List of Tables   ix

Preface   xi

Introduction: Definitions and Background   1

Part One
Rational Decision Making in U.S. Legislative Committee Systems   11

1   Understanding Individual Preferences in a Committee   13

2   The Internal Forces for Decentralized Agenda Setting in American Legislative Committee Systems   20

3   Party Leadership, Party Caucuses, and Standing Committees: Why Committee Outcomes Are Preferred in the United States   37

4   Does Decentralized Agenda Setting Pay Dividends?   52

Part Two
Lifestyle and Career-Pattern Influences   67

5   Costs and Benefits of Legislative Service   69

6   Self-Interest and Legislative Turnover   82

Part Three
Explorations in Efficiency and Reform   95

7   Risk, Efficiency, and Adaptation in Committee Decision Making   97

8   Committee System Optimalities: Size Preferences and Member Adaptation   106

9   Representation and the Reduction of Complexity in Lawmaking   122

10   The Complex Committee Game   143

Appendix: Survey Information   153

Bibliography   159

Index   165

Illustrations

3.1 Classification of State Chambers According to Importance of Party and Committee Decision Making.

4.1 Percentage of Legislator Responses Indicating Factional Conflict, by Representation of Their Parties in the Legislature.

5.1 Indifference (or Preference) Curves of "Citizen" and "Professional" Legislators.

7.1 Theoretical Relationship between Decision Costs and External Costs.

8.1 Decision/External Cost Functions for Varying Committee Sizes under Constant Decision Rule.

9.1 Relationship between Chamber Size and Four Committee System Characteristics.

10.1 Scenario for Sponsorship Success.

10.2 Counter-Scenario to Sponsorship Success.

Tables

2.1 Minimum Estimate of Bill Sponsorship Rate.

2.2 Tendency of Legislators to Sponsor Bills That Are Assigned to Their Own Committees.

2.3 Average Committee Size and Standard Deviation by Chamber (1981).

2.4 Successful Sponsorships: Percent Leading to Committee Approval or Enactment.

3.1 Influence of Majority Party Advantage and Chamber Size on Party and Committee Decision Making.

3.2 Satisfaction Ratings: Mean Differences between Party Caucus and Committees for Fifty Chambers in which Party Caucus Is Important.

3.3 Comparison of Majority and Minority Party Member Preferences for Committee versus Caucus Outcomes.

4.1 Number of House and Senate Bills Received by Each State Chamber, 1981, and Final Chamber Action.

4.2 Legislator Perceptions of Significant Decision-Making Loci (Frequencies).

4.3 Decision-Making Centralization Scores for State Legislative Chambers.

4.4 Identification of Committee System Problems.

4.5 Variables Affecting the Chamber Passage Rate.

5.1 Number of Workdays, 1981: State Legislative Chambers.

5.2 Majority Member Satisfaction Ratings of
Outcomes (Mean Scores).

6.1 Summary of Reasons for Voluntarily Vacating
Legislative Seat.

7.1 Committee Work Distributions in a Typical
Legislative Day.

8.1 Differences between Preferred and Actual
Committee Size (I–A1).

8.2 Differences between Preferred and Actual
Committee Size (I–A2).

8.3 Subcommittee Use and the Relationship between Actual
and Preferred Committee Size.

8.4 Large and Small Chamber and the Relationship between
Actual and Preferred Committee Size (1981).

8.5 Chamber Size, Subcommittee Use, and the Relationship
between Actual and Preferred Committee Size (1981).

8.6 Committee Attendance: Relationship to Actual Committee
Size and Preferred Committee Size.

8.7 Criticisms of Committee Systems by Senators in
Legislatures with Joint Committees and in
Other Legislatures.

9.1 Illustrative Cmin and Cmax Values for Increasing
Numbers of Members and Proposals.

9.2 Relationship between Committee Characteristics and
Time-Costs.

10.1 Relationship between Mean Number of Committee
Assignments and "Too Many Committee
Assignments" Complaint.

Preface

A realization that gained strength as this project unfolded is the extent to which the United States legislative committee system is an important organizational phenomenon. It is a critical form, I think, in the understanding of all organizations that practice collective choice. The United States Congress is often noted for its unique qualities, but an examination of the fifty state legislatures and ninety-nine chambers has led me to feel that organizationally Congress is unique only in minor ways, and that there is an evolutionary process in which commonly felt needs bring about similar changes. It seems apparent that many of the interesting theory-based propositions drawn from observations about Congressional behavior are testable at the state level by methods acceptable to the scientific community.

State legislative committee systems offer also an almost irresistible challenge to our understanding of how individuals behave rationally in a collective choice environment. They offer an opportunity to utilize theoretical elements of rational choice in conjunction with systematically collected evidence about ongoing organizational entities. The state legislative bodies serve almost as a "natural experiment." Many structural components are identical from state to state, yet in other ways state or chamber attributes vary considerably. Within different structural constraints, legislators employ trial and error to achieve their goals. They do so in different size chambers, in different size committees, in varying numbers of committees, perhaps in party caucuses, and perhaps in subcommittees. It would seem that discovering optimalities in the interplay of structure and behavior poses neither too great nor too small a challenge. In any case it is a challenge this book accepts.

Students of comparative state politics (as distinguished from national politics) have for a long time experienced serious deficiencies in regularized data collection. There is no national program to record or even consolidate state level data through the use of modern technology.

As scholars, we have been fortunate to have the Council of State Government publications to inform us of many of the basics, but I have found in every case in my own research that I must initiate additional surveys, not only for opinions of participants, but for basic facts that should be collected on a more systematic basis. For help in this regard I am grateful to the National Science Foundation and to the Weldon Springs Foundation of the University of Missouri. Their financial support was crucial.

While I am grateful for the financial support for this project, it should be stated that greater resources would have allowed more definitive and expansive work. To some I suppose this effort may seem broad enough, but several self-limiting choices had to be made. In writing the chapters of this book I hope to stimulate some of the additional research that I could not undertake. My primary data sources are the responses of over two thousand legislators to a fifty-state questionnaire, official and semi-official information received from legislative service personnel in all fifty states, and more complete information from two "case-study" states, Indiana and Missouri.

Many individuals were involved in this project, but I wish to thank most of all three co-authors, all of whom were funded at one time or another, and all of whom contributed greatly to the success of the project. James Riddlesperger worked with me at the inception of the study when it was funded by NSF. He successfully directed data collection operations for the main survey of state legislators while completing his graduate work. We co-authored "U.S. State Legislative Committees: Structure, Procedural Efficiency, and Party Control," *Legislative Studies Quarterly* 7 (1982): 453–71. Pieces of this article appear throughout the book.

The second co-author was William Jacoby, who came into the project in the analysis stages while he was completing his dissertation at North Carolina. His computer and statistical expertise and advice were invaluable. We also co-authored the piece "Scaling Legislative Decision-Making: A Methodological Exercise," *Political Behavior* 7 (1985): 285–303. The results of this article are employed in chapter five.

The third co-author, John R. Baker, came to the project nearer to its completion. While doing his graduate work, he directed new data collections to supplement the main legislator survey, including a special study of two states as well as additional fifty-state material. We co-authored "Why Do U.S. State Legislators Vacate Their Seats?" *Legislative Studies Quarterly* 11 (1986): 119–26. This article is incorporated, with only a few additions, into chapter seven under the title of "Self-Interest and Legislative Turnover."

The main legislator survey employed in this study was developed through two methods. First, I implemented a pilot survey prior to NSF funding. Second, NSF funding supported a panel of consultants for the final construction of the questionnaire. The survey and legislative specialist consultants were Ronald Hedlund, William Panning, Eric Uslaner, and Ronald Weber. Randall Calvert and Gary Miller were consulted for their mathematical expertise and rational choice interests. While the final decisions were mine, their assistance was very beneficial and I am grateful for their help. I can recommend the procedure to other researchers.

During the several years of this project's existence, sound advice and help have come from a variety of sources. In particular, I wish to thank John Freeman for his mathematical advice when the ideas for the work were germinating, Jim King for his help with the survey and discussions about the content, and several other colleagues who have offered helpful criticisms on parts of the project, including Keith Hamm and Malcolm Jewell.

I am indebted also to Wendy Francis, a mathematics major at the University of Texas, who helped with the coding and was able to construct a needed proof (where her father had failed). Others who worked diligently on the project were Barbara Cable, Rob Presley, and Deborah Basnett, all undergraduate students at the time.

Introduction:
Definitions and Background

Committees and Committee Systems

The foremost feature of the "legislative committee game" is that it is played within a committee *system*. Yet not very much can be said about a "committee system" without first discussing a single committee. A "committee" in popular usage may refer to a group of people selected by any means for any purpose to conduct business in any manner whatsoever. Committees are formed by election, appointment, or even self-selection. Many committees are purely advisory in nature, providing information or acting as sounding boards. Many so-called committees are no more than collections of individuals who meet at the request of an executive. Committees often never vote or even provide evidence of collective action.

In his well-known work, *The Theory of Committees and Elections,* Duncan Black refers to a committee as a "group of people who arrive at a decision by means of voting" (Black, 1958, p. 1). His definition allows him to treat elections and electorates in the context of committees. The subject of this book is more focused; it concerns only *face-to-face* groups of people who arrive at decisions through voting. An electorate may be seen as a committee, but a legislature or parliament is almost always a face-to-face committee, selected by an electorate.

For convenience of expression, a legislature need not be called a committee except to make a point. Its principal units of organization are "committees," and committees have subcommittees. Furthermore, legislatures have political party units, which are also committees, and many legislatures have an assortment of other units that could qualify as committees. As long as they vote to make decisions, they are committees. But for most narrative purposes, it will be appropriate to employ distinctive labels such as caucus, standing committee, chamber, or legislature.

A committee system is a set of committees whose decisions, at least in part, are interdependent. Among the more complex committee systems are those that govern nations or their subdivisions, namely, legislative committee systems. Interdependence in legislative committee systems manifests itself in a number of ways:

> The parent committee, the legislature, dissolves into standing committees, which in turn may dissolve into subcommittees.
>
> Decisions of subcommittees are subject to review by the standing committees and their decisions in turn are subject to review by the entire chamber.
>
> Committees frequently have overlapping jurisdictions and memberships, and members of different committees may find it necessary to trade or bargain both within and across committee jurisdictions.
>
> The party caucus intervenes before and/or after the decisions of standing committees in many legislatures, either setting the agenda for standing committees, or preparing positions and agenda for floor action.
>
> In many legislatures an executive committee (or policy committee) will attempt to set guidelines for other committee units.

In essence and in most instances, a national or state legislature is a committee system.

In many legislative committee systems, a rich if not overwhelming array of committees has been created. In addition to the normal duty of processing legislation, their tasks range from minor housekeeping functions to such activities as raising campaign money, resolving chamber differences, and meeting with the chief executive. *This book will focus upon those committees that actually process legislation:* mainly the chambers, the standing committees and their subcommittees, and the party caucuses.

The Central Role of Standing Committees in American Legislatures

In American legislatures, the standing committees and their subcommittees serve as the principal organizational units for processing legislation. Nevertheless, until recently both systematic empirical investigation and the development of theory relating to standing committees have been rare (Uslaner and Weber, 1977, p. 433; Eulau and McCluggage, 1984, p. 200). As Eulau and McCluggage have further noted, only two early works stand out: the insightful tirade of Woodrow Wilson against standing committees in the House of Representatives in his *Congressional Government* (1885), and the lesser known but more systematic work of Lauros McConachie in *Congressional Committees* (1898).

Studies of standing committees in American legislatures have flourished since the 1950s, most notably in the study of Congress, beginning in 1954 with Ralph Huitt's "The Congressional Committee: A Case Study," referred to as "pathbreaking" by Eulau and McCluggage. The sheer complexity of Congress has no doubt stimulated many scholars to focus on a single committee. The better examples include analyses of the House Appropriations Committee (Fenno, 1962), the House Ways and Means Committee (Manley, 1965), and the House Public Works Committee (Murphy, 1974). A comparison of six committees (Appropriations, Ways and Means, Interior, Post Office, Education and Labor, and Foreign Affairs) was also completed by Fenno in 1973, and a multi-committee treatment of public works issues was completed by Ferejohn in 1974. Among the benefits derived from these studies is the in-depth look at committees with subcommittees (except Ways and Means). While subcommittees in Congress appear to have arisen as a postbellum phenomenon in the expansion of Congressional duties (McConachie, pp. 135–137), it is only recently that they threaten preeminence in lawmaking.

For state legislatures, studies of single standing committees do not have the luxury of prima facie importance in the scholarly community. No doubt many excellent studies are buried, perhaps never to be unearthed, in the dust of dissertation libraries. As a consequence, or perhaps in any case, the historical record on the internal structure and operation of state standing committees is at best scattered. About the only early work of any breadth was completed by C. I. Winslow in 1931.

Winslow's study provides overall statistical data for every state standing committee structure (number of committees, size of committees, number of committee assignments) and makes a special study of Pennsylvania and Maryland, where he found that standing committee action on bills was the final action in over 80 percent of the cases. Repeated surveys since 1963 (Francis, 1967; Uslaner and Weber, 1977; Francis and Riddlesperger, 1982) have made it clear that standing committees in state legislatures are very important centers of decision making. In a related multistate work, Rosenthal (1974) gave principal weight to the attributes of standing committees in his assessment of legislative performance in the states.

Relatively little is known about "standing committees" in the legislatures of other nations. First, it is evident that where they exist they are not nearly as vital to their governments as those of Congress are to the U.S. government. Second, their lack of importance has no doubt reduced the quantity of scholarship on the subject. Third, given the late start of political science as a discipline, even allowing for its rapid growth in the United States, it is not surprising that we have only very recently learned very much of comparative value (See Mezey, 1979; Lees and Shaw, 1979; Olson, 1980). We might conjecture that "standing committees" in parliamentary bodies have been less attractive to their members for two reasons: (1) The ability of members to obtain cabinet posts, which dilutes their interest in forming strong committees, and (2) the fears of the leadership that strong committees would only further fragment what is already a multiparty system.

Institutionalization

A related perspective may be drawn from Nelson Polsby's examination of institutionalization of the U.S. House of Representatives (1968). To Polsby, an organization becomes institutionalized when it: (1) becomes differentiated from its environment by developing and channeling career opportunities; (2) develops a division of labor in which roles are specified; and (3) becomes universalistic rather than particularistic in its methods of conducting internal business (p. 145). The first two criteria are intimately tied to the standing committees and their subcommittees. Committee and subcommittee positions are made increasingly attractive to members as they acquire greater seniority. And the division of labor in Congress is mostly one of dividing up the work among the various standing committees and their subcommittees.

The institutionalization of Congress may be seen as an evolutionary process. Within the U.S. Constitutional framework, where legislators aspire to committee headships rather than cabinet posts, organizational development and elaboration will occur in the standing committee and subcommittee structure. It would appear that Congress has been driven also by the need to adapt to increasing demands for action in an increasingly complex and technical society. As society becomes more specialized, so must Congress, if it is to govern.

Specialization in society is reflected in the pressures brought to bear by organized interest groups and also by the growth and differentiation of the federal bureaucracy. Congress has responded to the increased demands for action and the need to control first by allowing itself to dissolve into standing committees, and then by allowing those committees to unfold into subcommittees. In sum, *careerism* and the *need to specialize* have stimulated institutionalization along the lines suggested. There is debate, of course, over whether or not these developments are desirable (Lowi, 1964; Ripley and Franklin, 1984; Dodd and Oppenheimer, 1981).

A cross national perspective might well lead to the conclusion that Congress is unique, but an examination of the fifty U.S. state legislatures would suggest just the opposite—not that Congress is indistinguishable, for it certainly does possess features unmatched in the states. Nevertheless, in almost every important way relating to structure and development, most of the states' legislatures are similar to Congress. To locate these similarities, it is important to examine the structure of the committee *system* which includes both chambers and the party caucuses, as well as the standing committees and their subcommittees.

In the twentieth century, the state legislatures have been slower to institutionalize. It is only in recent years that most state legislatures have met annually rather than once every two years. With annual sessions have come longer sessions as well. Many states have witnessed an evolution from part-time to full-time duty and, with it, increased "careerism"—legislators who list their occupation as "legislator" rather than salesman, realtor, teacher or retailer. On the surface it does appear that the state legislatures are following a path of development similar to that of Congress. This possibility has been noted, with some reservations, by Chaffey (1970) in his comparison of the Montana and Wisconsin legislatures.

Although it is difficult to show empirically, most observers of state legislative politics would probably agree that subcommittee use has become much more common since 1960. Not a single remark about subcommittees has been found in the literature of state politics dating to 1970, although by this time the "bill explosion" (Rosenthal and Forth, 1978) no doubt had spawned the use of subcommittees in the busier standing committees; and there is no question that a thorough search would turn up earlier evidence of subcommittee use also. In a 1981 survey, however, respondents from approximately two-thirds of the chambers indicated frequent subcommittee use (Francis and Riddlesperger, 1982). It is doubtful that they were ever so common before. In sum, the state legislatures appear to be developing and institutionalizing along Congressional lines, a process that includes further differentiation of the committee system.

Individuals in Committees

A social science theory of a committee system cannot progress very far without making inferences about individual preferences. Of course there are different methods for making inferences. A favorite tool of the theoretician is to make an *assumption* about human preference. The assumption is based normally upon introspection or observation and may or may not be directly verifiable. For example, it is often assumed that members of Congress seek reelection. We know that not all prefer reelection (Cooper and West, 1981), but assuming that most do helps explain many other activities in Congress (Mayhew, 1974; Fenno, 1973; Kingdon, 1977; Fiorina, 1977).

Inferences about human preferences can be derived from a number of empirical methods as well. Experimental research can be helpful (e.g., Fiorina and Plott, 1978), but since committee behavior is uniquely human—one never encounters a committee of mammals— very few legislative scholars apparently have found such work cost-efficient. Most of the empirical research on legislatures has been nonexperimental, derived from direct observation, interviews, questionnaires, and official documents. Many legislators have been asked about their preferences through interviews and questionnaires. Included are state comparative studies of role orientations (Wahlke, *et al.*, 1962), policy preferences (Uslaner and Weber, 1977), and committee organizational preferences (Francis and Riddlesperger, 1982; Francis, 1985a). Included also are many studies of Congress. Especially pertinent to committees is Shepsle's study of "revealed preferences"—actual freshman requests for committee assignments in the House of Representatives for the Eighty-sixth through the Ninety-third Congresses (1978).

In political situations there are several ways individuals attempt to satisfy their preferences—through the use or threat of force, through delegating, through trading or bargaining, through voting, or through the use of information. Since committee systems in this book are democratic institutions, only the latter four will be of concern. Legislators delegate responsibilities, trade and bargain over legislation, vote on proposals, and seek or use information to accomplish their goals in a variety of ways. A principal goal of a legislator is to get his or her way on legislation, and it is in this game of legislating that these instruments of decision making come into sharp focus.

From an organizational perspective, the act of *delegating* is the most critical instrument of decision making. Delegating is an act that transfers decision-making authority or responsibility from one set of individuals to a differently composed set. Through delegating, members can determine in part how trading and bargaining will occur, who will vote and on what issues, and the nature of information that will be available. Delegating involves moving people around, which in turn affects how individuals will apply the other instruments of decision making.

Most delegations of authority in legislatures involve *contingencies*. For example, the scope of responsibilities of the group to whom they are delegated may be limited. Also certain internal decision-making rules, such as majority rule, may be imposed. In addition, policy controls over the decisions of the group may be retained (as when the entire chamber must approve a bill reported out of a standing committee). In practice, a number of puzzling questions arise in this process. How should the responsibilities be divided? How much autonomy should be given to the delegated groups? What standards of conduct should be enforced? It is necessary also to determine who shall serve in such groups or committees. The committee assignment process in Congress, for example, has become a major topic of research (for review, see Eulau, 1984).

In face-to-face committees, where voting is required to arrive at decisions, *trading or bargaining* seems inevitable. Winning majority support requires members to be flexible in their recommendations. A legislative proposal has its supporters and opponents, but in the middle are those members who are opposed unless certain amendments are accepted. Members may bargain also by trading support over two separate proposals. In either situation, it can be shown that members of committees, for strategic reasons, often find it rational to *not* vote their true preferences (Farquarson, 1969; Brams, 1975, chap. 2, 4).

The *use of information* is a crucial factor in understanding the behavior of members in committees. Members seek to consume information for personal advantage or benefit in a variety of ways. They want to know about the content of proposals and their implications. They want to know about the preferences of other members. And they want to know about the preferences of people outside the committee. *Information search and consumption* are important for individual decision making. Also important is the *communication of information*. One way that individuals can change the behavior of others is to provide them with new information. In this sense, specialization and expertise carry influence. The expert or specialist in an area is in a better position to contribute to the information pool.

Information costs are substantial in legislative committee systems. Legislators have many decisions to make, and they are inundated with information regarding those decisions. Reports from bureaucrats, lobbyists, media outlets, and legislative staff are plentiful in most legislatures. It is usually the quality not the quantity of information that is lacking. As Anthony Downs has made clear, the search for and consumption of information is a costly enterprise and the rational actor must feel that the benefits will outweigh the costs (1957, pp. 207–276). The legislator is a "best case" example of Herbert A. Simon's principle of "bounded rationality," expressed in the assertion that

> The capacity of the human mind for formulating and solving complex problems is very small compared with the size of the problems whose solution is required for objectively rational behavior in the real world—or even for a reasonable approximation to such objective rationality. (1957, p. 198)

As Simon would have it, legislators can be expected to engage in *satisficing* rather than maximizing behavior in the pursuit of information.

Individual Behavior and Committee Structure

A long-standing assumption in human affairs is that organizational structure affects individual behavior. From an international perspective U.S. legislatures may seem organizationally similar, but the members do work under a variety of structural conditions (Hedland, 1984). Perhaps most distinct are the great differences in obligation, from full-time service in Congress and such states as California, to minimal part-time service in the least populated states. The committee systems vary substantially also, with great differences in the number of standing committees, the size of standing committees, the use of subcommittees, the importance of the party caucus, the number of bills the committees process, and so forth. The extent to which such differences affect individual behavior can serve as a basis for theory development in legislative organization.

The legislative environment may be seen as a continuous interplay

between institutional structure or procedure and individual adjustment
and adaptation. The most important stress between structure and behavior in American legislatures appears to be the great demand for legislative action. The volume of demand for action exceeds the ability of
most legislatures to supply the time and energy to respond. Normal processes of representation (e.g., full deliberation, amending, voting) are
often incompatible with swiftness of action. The fifty state legislatures
offer an excellent opportunity to better understand the tensions that arise
when legislators intend not to ratify, but to legislate.

Organization of Chapters

The next five chapters of this book are devoted to developing an understanding of rational decision making in U.S. legislative committee systems, beginning with the logic of individual behavior in a single
committee, and ending with general questions of payoff and reward.
Chapter one contains an introduction to the formal language and notation employed in more complex ways later in the book. Such material is
presented within the context of a single committee, and it needs to be
mastered before encountering a number of sections in other chapters. It
is important to have a formal way of representing human preferences;
otherwise, it becomes difficult if not impossible to assess the impact of
institutional rules and structure upon human preferences, and to know
how preferences relate to voting and agenda setting.

In chapter two, the first chapter in which data are analyzed, a number of arguments are put forth relating to the distribution of agenda setting, committee assignment accommodation, and sponsorship success.
An empirical basis is established to illustrate the relationship of individual choice to legislative procedure and the existence of decentralized
agenda setting. It is this relationship that serves as a central theme of the
book. Chapter three balances the notion of decentralized commit-
tee/subcommittee decision making with party leadership and party caucus decision making. Do legislators prefer standing committee decision
outcomes to caucus outcomes? Chapter four raises the natural follow-up
question of whether decentralized agenda setting pays dividends in the
passage of legislation. A series of regression experiments are performed
to answer this question.

Chapters five and six are devoted to broader concerns relating to the
influence of legislative lifestyle and career patterns. Chapter five ex-

plores the extent to which the passage of legislation (or the passage rate) and the number of legislative workdays in the state capitol lead to overall legislator satisfaction with outcomes. To what extent do opportunity costs in the private sector offset benefits obtained in the public performance of duties? In the final chapter of part two (chapter six), a review of the legislative turnover literature is provided together with a recent evaluation of legislative retirements in two states. Career patterns are changing in the state legislatures, and these changes may have an impact on legislator incentives for internal reorganization and efficiency.

One of the more important conclusions resulting from the analysis provided in parts one and two of this book is that procedural efficiency is probably highly valued by most legislators. This may seem odd to many consumers of media commentary and coverage. Legislative inefficiency is a frequent accusation of frustrated chief executives and others who want particular results. Part three of this book is designed to explore methods of increasing procedural efficiency within legislative organizations.

In chapter seven a number of conceptual distinctions are introduced. Legislators are motivated, it is assumed, to reduce risks and to reduce decision costs. But these are not necessarily compatible goals. Are there optimal ways of organizing to minimize risks and costs? In chapter eight the notion of an "optimal committee system" is developed. Legislator survey results on committee structure are assessed in relationship to subcommittee use and chamber size. To what extent are legislators able to adapt to structural inefficiencies?

A major source of risky and costly decision making may be found in the "complexity of decision making." How do legislators cope with complexity? Chapter nine assumes that legislators cope with complexity by finding ways of reducing it. Complexity is created in part by the sheer volume of legislation, and in part by the interpersonal nature of collective choice decision making. Legislators can reduce complexity by making appropriate committee organizational decisions. This chapter links the structure of preferences to committee organization in order to better understand efficiency requirements.

The final chapter describes a "scenario" for sponsorship success. There is also a counter scenario for sponsorship success. These two scenarios correspond to "efficient" and "inefficient" procedure in the processing of legislation. They are keys to understanding the way in which the legislative committee game is played.

Part One

Rational Decision Making in U.S. Legislative Committee Systems

1

Understanding Individual Preferences in a Committee

The preferences of members of a single committee might seem fairly easy to comprehend. There is a literature, however, that attests to the superficiality of this view. The theoretical intricacies of game theory and social choice theory, the implications of the need for multidimensional scaling of attitudes, and the inability to account for a high level of variance in most statistical models of human choice, all serve to point out complexity of human preference rather than simplicity. Nevertheless, the purpose of this chapter is to offer a way of comprehending individual behavior in the legislative context of a single committee in order to better understand behavior in the context of a committee "system." To do so, we can first take up those restrictions or constraints most common to legislative committees and then we can explore the flexibilities within those constraints.

Jurisdictional and Time Constraints

Entire legislatures can have broad jurisdictions, but they are still limited by national boundaries, higher levels of government, or constitutional sanctions. The standing committees and subcommittees of legislatures, of course, have more limited jurisdictions. For each standing committee, only certain kinds of issues are eligible for action, and these issues appear in the form of proposals, mainly bills or amendments to bills. For most legislative committees, the input of issues either in the form of bills or amendments to bills is open rather than fixed, subject mainly to the time available to consider them. *Jurisdictional limits and available time act as two major constraints upon the introduction of issues and their consideration.*

Voting Procedures

For the study of legislatures, a number of procedural assumptions are appropriate to most if not all situations. Among the most common rules of procedure are *majority rule* and *binary voting*. In tallying the vote, stated preferences of members are counted equally within the committee, and the alternative receiving the highest count is declared the winning alternative. The preferences are almost always registered in the form of "preference to pass" some measure or "preference to defeat" it. Those whose preferences are counted consist of all members of the committee, or of all of those actually present to be counted.

Within the above framework, there are two distinct voting procedures, the *amendment* procedure, and the *successive* voting procedure (as made explicit in Farquharson, 1969; Brams, 1975). In the amendment procedure, the practice is to put forward a primary proposal that will be voted on after one or more possible modifications through amendment. In the successive voting procedure, proposals are introduced independently and disposed of one at a time. In most legislative situations, however, more than one proposal will be in the hopper at any given time, and members will have knowledge of what proposals are ready for consideration. In many cases amendments also are filed in advance of meetings, a tendency that increases perhaps with institutionalization and formality.

Saliency, Separability, and Preference Maps

To each member of a committee, the issues that come before it will have varying degrees of *saliency*. In other words, the member will want to win on some issues more than on others. For example, suppose that two bills were up for consideration, bills 35 and 36. A legislator may prefer to win on bill 35 more than on 36, in which case we can state:

$$W(35) > W(36)$$

where ">" substitutes for the phrase "is preferred to." To the legislator in question, bill 35 is more salient than bill 36.

Since legislative committees utilize binary voting, in the sense that all members vote for pass or fail, our representation of member preferences need not be any more complex. Thus, if a member prefers that a bill *pass* rather than be *defeated*, we can state his preference:

$$P > D$$

If the member prefers that both bills 35 and 36 pass, his preferences may be represented as follows:

$$W(35) > W(36)$$
$$P \qquad P$$

where $P > D$ is implied in each case.

Still we have an incomplete map of the individual's preferences. Further elaboration requires that we ask which of the remaining possible outcomes (PD, DP, DD) the member prefers and in what order. A full display of possible outcomes might produce:

$$W(35) > W(36)$$

P	P	Most preferred outcome
P	D	Second preferred outcome
D	P	Third preferred outcome
D	D	Least preferred outcome

In this example, the member prefers both bills to pass, but short of that he would prefer that bill 35 pass. If bill 35 does not pass he would still prefer that bill 36 pass. The least desirable outcome occurs when both bills are defeated.

The example as it is constructed above represents preferences on two issues for a single individual. In this instance, the preferences on the two issues are *separable*; that is, preferences on one issue are not contingent upon the fate of the second issue. In contrast, the preferences in the following example are *inseparable*:

$$W(35) > W(36)$$

P	P	Most Preferred Outcome
D	D	Second Preferred Outcome
P	D	Third Preferred Outcome
D	P	Least Preferred Outcome

If bill 35 promotes banks and bill 36 promotes savings and loans firms, the above preferences suggest that the member most prefers to aid both types of financial institutions (PP). However, if either bill does not pass, he would prefer the other not to pass also (DD) in order to preserve fair competition between banks and their savings and loans rivals. If neither of these outcomes is possible (both pass or both are defeated), he would still favor banks (PD) over savings and loans (DP).

Situations that illustrate separable and inseparable preferences are common in legislatures. Unrelated bills normally will yield separable preferences unless such preferences become inseparable because of log-rolling or bargaining. Inseparable preferences are expressed often in relation to appropriations and pork barrel legislation. At the state level, for example, it is common for a legislator to oppose an increase in funding for the state university system unless the state four-year college system is given a similar increase. In Congress, the omnibus bill is a classic example of inseparable preferences run amuck (Ferejohn, 1974).

The *preference maps* illustrated in the above examples cover positions on two issues only. Such maps may be extended to any number of issues or proposals, with the number of possible outcomes increasing exponentially, or 2^M where M is the number of proposals. Thus three proposals yield eight possible outcomes, and four proposals offer sixteen possibilities. The preference maps become very complex very quickly as new proposals are added to the matrix. For three proposals only, a legislator might rank the outcomes in order of preference as follows:

> PPD   Most Preferred Outcome
> PPP
> PDD
> PDP
> DPD
> DPP
> DDD
> DDP   Least Preferred Outcome

This is only one of 8! (the factorial) different rankings of these eight preference alternatives.

Changing Preferences and Votes

Legislators do change their preferences and votes. A most common cause is the introduction of new information. Legislators are exposed to a great deal of information about the content and consequences of specific proposals, and they also learn about who does and does not support each proposal. Such information frequently will change the preferences of members, and often their votes as well. It is estimated, for example, that state legislators spend an average of two hours a day obtaining information about proposals in their committees and another hour finding out how other members feel about the issues (Francis and Riddlesperger, 1982).

Members may change their votes without changing their preferences. Events of this kind occur when legislators become involved in vote trading. A member votes for a colleague's proposal only because a reciprocal vote-favor is expected on another measure. Votes are at best "revealed" preferences, which may or may not correspond to "true" preferences. Along these lines it is customary to distinguish between "sincere" voting and "sophisticated" voting, where it is implied that sincere voting expresses true preferences in disregard of strategic considerations. Sophisticated voting, in contrast, represents the calculation of a winning vote strategy in relation to some larger goal (Farquharson, 1969; Riker & Ordeshook, 1973).

Sophisticated voting occurs when members estimate that preferences of others on the issues are inseparable. For example, if an attempt is made to include funding for a new optometry school in the higher education bill, the sponsor of the higher education bill might vote against his own wishes in support of optometry funding in order to preserve majority support for the remainder of the general bill. If he thought that other members would vote their original intentions, uninfluenced by the optometry amendment, then there would be no need to cast a sophisticated vote. It might be noted that the sophisticated vote is very much like a vote-trade, except that there is no concrete transaction.

Setting the Agenda

There are two major reasons why setting the agenda is so important in legislative committees. First, the order in which issues are taken up makes a difference in the way members vote. Second, due to the crowded agenda, many issues at the tail end will never be considered. While these observations may seem obvious, it will be helpful here to clarify their theoretical and practical underpinnings.

When we examine the true preferences of individuals with respect to a set of proposals, it will be found that *if* the preferences are *separable*, the individuals will choose to vote the same way on each proposal regardless of the order in which the proposals are decided. As each new issue comes up, the members need not regret their previous votes. The issues can be separable in both the amendment procedure and the successive voting procedure. A member who offers a bill enforcing the use of automobile seatbelts, for example, may prefer that it pass with or without proposed amendments that would alter the severity of the penalty. The outcome of that entire issue may have no effect upon the member's position on a toxic waste law.

The neatness of separable preferences can be thwarted, however, by members who logroll or *vote trade* on the issues. Opponents of the seatbelt law might change their vote to support it in exchange for other members' support on the toxic waste bill. In such a case, the opponents might decide to vote for the toxic waste bill if and only if the seatbelt bill is passed. In the same manner, the amendment process can be altered by trades in which, for example, a member agrees to support the amendment of a colleague in exchange for support of his own amendment. It is evident that such trades require an element of "trust," and that the order of the agenda is relevant to the interested parties. A member would prefer to have the bill most salient to him appear first.

Vote trading can have the affect of making separable preferences inseparable, but it is very likely that many of the preferences over proposed legislation are inseparable in the first place. The most preferred outcome on one issue will depend on the fate of another issue. When preferences are inseparable, the order of the agenda is a crucial matter. The beauty of the amendment process is that members are able to insert their most preferred alternative (the bill with an amendment) at the top of the agenda prior to voting on a much less preferred alternative (the bill without the amendment). As one would expect, legislators frequently are opposed to legislation unless their own amendments are accepted. Such amendments at the same time may turn others against the legislation.

The ramifications of agenda setting in this context can be seen vividly in Congress. Ferejohn's 1974 evaluation of public works projects in the Omnibus Rivers and Harbors and Flood Control Bill of 1968 paints a convincing picture of how bills win acceptance in standing committees—by allocating projects to the states of committee members. Although the projects are not necessarily inserted by formal amendment, it is in fact the formal power of amendment and vote that encourages a distribution of benefits among committee or subcommittee members. In contrast, we might note how the Committee of the Whole conducts its business on the floor of the House. Normally, the leadership adopts a highly restrictive amendment policy because it thinks that majority support has been achieved. Further amendment might well destabilize the coalition. As Riker and Ordeshook (1973; p. 100) have pointed out, the amendment process does allow manipulation through the introduction of paradoxes (i.e., cyclical majorities).

The order in which legislation is considered is important not only in the amendment process but also in the processing of separate bills. The vote of a legislator on one bill may depend upon the outcome of another bill. A state legislator may feel the need to increase state revenue, and if that feeling is broadly shared, there will probably be several bills proposing tax increases. The legislator may prefer most an increase in the sales tax only but, failing that, he or she may prefer an increase supported by one of the other measures. For strategic reasons, the legislator may prefer to vote on the sales tax increase first, calculating that if it passes, the other measures will not be successful.

In sum, it can be seen from the above that preferences may be inseparable either because of vote trading or the actual nature of original preferences, and that such conditions may exist in both the amendment process and the successive voting procedure. Whenever preferences are *inseparable*, the order of the agenda is important. It is difficult to know just how often inseparable preferences characterize members' positions, but it seems clear that the phenomenon is common if not dominant.

Finally, it is apparent that under the busy conditions of many legislatures, much legislation is never given serious consideration. Moving legislation to a formal hearing may be more difficult for a legislator than getting it approved once a hearing is granted. In this context, the formal organization of the legislature becomes very important. The efficiency with which legislative proposals are processed will have a bearing on the extent to which rank-and-file members are able to act effectively in the pursuit of their own favored legislation. In practical terms, in most American legislatures, this type of efficiency is affected by the standing committee and subcommittee structure and associated chamber rules.

2

The Internal Forces for Decentralized Agenda Setting in American Legislative Committee Systems

The argument can be made that standing committees in American legislatures are created to serve the goals of majority party leaders (Liebowitz and Tollison, 1980). The argument assumes that majority party leaders have an agenda and that they seek to maximize the number of agenda items that receive favorable action. Since the available hearing time for agenda items is usually insufficient to consider every leadership agenda item in full forum, the leaders will prefer to create committees to expedite the processing of legislation. The committees can handle legislation simultaneously, and floor action can be limited to little more than a simple ratification of committee decisions. In this sense leaders may find it rational to "manage by committee."

An alternative argument is that standing committees are created instead to satisfy the demands of rank-and-file legislators. Each member of the legislature has an agenda (changing and overlapping), and each member seeks to maximize the success of his or her agenda. When it is evident that a full forum of the legislature can consider only a small fraction of the total number of items on the agenda of N members, most of the members will favor the creation of standing committees. Those least likely to favor the committees will be those with the greatest ability to get their issues on the front end of the agenda. By this reasoning the majority party leaders would be the most resistant to standing committees.

While the second argument appears to run contrary to the Liebowitz-Tollison thesis, the contradiction can be resolved by assuming, as most observers would, that the legislative "game" is not in any strict sense a "zero-sum" game. There are benefits in excess of costs to be had by all, or at least by a majority. The party leaders need the committee system to process their agenda, and perhaps the rank-and-file members need it even more. When legislatures do form committees, it is an open question whether they are formed as concessions to rank-and-file members or as masterpieces of leadership strategy.

Two Leadership Approaches

The first type of leadership management, put forth in a thesis by Liebowitz and Tollison, implies that the majority leaders have more than a limited interest in efficiently expediting legislation and that they would prefer a system just efficient enough to secure passage of their own agendas. To do this they need to form coalitions with the appropriate committee chairs and to have supporters on key standing committees. Beyond that, it could be in the interest of the leaders to tolerate a highly cumbersome structure through which will filter only those items that are placed at the front end of the agenda. A congested schedule and a chair-dominated committee agenda would seem to advance leadership interests.

In a second type of management, the leaders build coalitions by honoring as many members' requests for chair appointments and committee assignments as possible—without any intent by leadership to block the proposals of colleagues. In fact, the intent is much in the spirit of "universalism" and "reciprocity" (Weingast, 1979; Shepsle and Weingast, 1981). The omnibus bill may have a piece for everyone, and what the committee produces the committee gets. In Lowi's sense of the term, the committees or subcommittees make the "distributive" decisions. In return, the party leaders may get their way on major redistributive and regulatory issues. As Weingast has shown under reasonable assumptions, winning coalitions are *not* stable and the un-

certainties of pure majority rule politics may lead members to prefer a
system with greater stability. Such a system is one where the norm of
reciprocity prevails.[1]

In spite of the likelihood that both leaders and followers will prefer
that standing committees process legislation, there is a natural tension
that arises because of widespread membership demands to influence the
agenda. The remainder of this analysis explores both the logic of individual choice and the weight of empirical evidence leading to or suggesting decentralized agenda setting. While much of the earlier work in
this area has focused on Congress, data in this analysis are drawn primarily from state legislative sources.

The Rank-and-File Perspective

Liebowitz and Tollison suggested that an appropriate goal of a party
leader is to maximize the passage *rate* of proposals on his or her
agenda, where say, $P = w/m$, the number of wins divided by the number of personal agenda items. It is evident, however, that the number of
wins is not as important as the value of the wins, or $U(w)$, and that in
fact a legislator would attempt to maximize $U(w)$ rather than w/m. The
question then becomes one of determining how a legislator goes about
maximizing $U(w)$. One way to do it is first to guarantee that all personal
agenda items will at least be considered. Liebowitz and Tollison cor-
rectly suggest that the leaders need a committee system to guarantee
consideration.

The same reasoning applies to rank-and-file members. They want
to maximize the number of personal agenda items considered because
doing so will increase the total value of their wins. Even more so than
the party leaders, rank-and-file members will find the goal of maximizing personal agenda consideration particularly attractive. Such a goal
can be fulfilled largely through early organizational decisions to expe-

---

1. The notion of *reciprocity* as it is used in this study refers to mutual accommodation
among members, both explicit and implicit, ranging from obvious vote swapping to
understandings that require no visible negotiations. Most of the empirical and theoretical
predecessors on this topic focus on the U.S. Congress, beginning perhaps with the study
of U.S. Senate folkways by Matthews (1960), the work of Clapp (1964), the analysis of
"distributive, regulatory, and redistributive" decision loci by Lowi (1964), Fenno's study
of the House Appropriations Committee (1962) and Ferejohn's study of rivers and harbors
legislation (1974). At the state level, reciprocity has been examined also (e.g., Wahlke et
al., 1962) but generally only in relation to the identification of norms.

dite bill processing. In the battle to get one's agenda accepted, there is a *two-step strategy*. The first step is to get as many items considered as possible through early favorable organizational decisions, including committee assignments. The second step is to fight harder for those items that have greater utility.

Do rank-and-file members have an agenda? Everyone has served on committees where they do not. But the modern national and state legislatures in the United States are thriving law production centers, and typically only the unusual legislator lacks an agenda. Generally, such an agenda is reflected in bill sponsorship—not completely nor precisely, but enough so that a sponsorship index for most legislative chambers can be highly reflective of what legislators are doing.

As suggestive examples we can examine a number of part-time legislatures, where one might expect that there would be more legislators without a sponsorship agenda. In a recent study of the lower chambers of South Carolina and Texas during the 1977 sessions, it was found that only 6.8 percent and 1.3 percent, respectively, did not serve as first author of legislation (Hamm, et al., 1983). In the 1981 sessions of Indiana and Missouri, senate sponsorship was distributed among almost all members, such that:

	Indiana	Missouri
Number of Members in Chamber	49	33
Number who Sponsored Bills	49	32
Number of Sponsorships per Member (Mean)	25.7	15.1

In the larger house chambers of each state we find a similar pattern:

	Indiana	Missouri
Number of Members in Chamber	99	163
Number who Sponsored Bills	97	148
Number of Sponsorships per Member (Mean)	11.7	6.1

The above information applies only to *bills in the house of origin* and each bill is identified as having one or two principal sponsors. Many members will sponsor legislation sent over from the other chamber, and in states such as Missouri many members other than the first and second "author" will sign on as sponsor. In other words, the mean sponsorship values above are probably low estimates in these states.

The point of the above examples is not to claim that the sponsorship

Table 2.1 Minimum Estimate of Bill Sponsorship Rate (Number of Bills Introduced in Chamber of Origin Divided by the Number of Members in Chamber).

State	House	Senate	State	House	Senate
Alabama	10.86	19.09	Montana	8.76	9.72
Alaska	26.28	51.85	Nebraska	11.47	
Arizona	8.27	13.67	Nevada	17.75	35.85
Arkansas	10.18	17.97	New Hampshire	2.40	13.61
California	28.79	32.03	New Jersey	10.59	14.37
Colorado	9.60	14.91	New Mexico	10.33	11.62
Connecticut	15.96	41.80	New York	62.17	120.17
Delaware	11.85	18.29	North Carolina	11.63	15.44
Florida	9.94	27.38	North Dakota	6.75	8.82
Georgia	6.37	8.18	Ohio	8.08	12.30
Hawaii	38.08	85.24	Oklahoma	4.72	7.56
Idaho	6.61	6.80	Oregon	22.80	34.20
Illinois	11.37	21.58	Pennsylvania	13.46	34.50
Indiana	11.45	10.12	Rhode Island	14.24	23.80
Iowa	8.78	11.58	South Carolina	6.60	10.48
Kansas	4.87	12.08	South Dakota	5.47	7.09
Kentucky	8.33	10.63	Tennessee	14.55	44.12
Louisiana	18.28	28.97	Texas	16.13	41.71
Maine	7.95	13.15	Utah	5.40	10.66
Maryland	14.32	25.49	Vermont	3.30	6.23
Massachusetts	46.80	61.45	Virginia	18.37	21.15
Michigan	12.45	16.05	Washington	7.70	27.84
Minnesota	11.49	22.03	West Virginia	11.00	21.14
Mississippi	12.43	21.77	Wisconsin	11.85	25.70
Missouri	5.54	13.88	Wyoming	8.73	8.53

data can be taken at face value, for it is well known that outside sponsors are important, and furthermore that in some states, measurement is confused by committee sponsorship or other unusual practices. The point to be made is that most members have a sponsorship agenda. If getting one's bills passed isn't the name of the game, it is certainly an important part of the game.

The collection of individual sponsorship information is a tedious and costly enterprise and will need to be expanded in future work. One can infer the *minimum* sponsorship rate, however, by knowing the number of bills and the number of members, since the bills in every state must have sponsors who are legislators. Table 2.1 illustrates bills per member for each chamber, utilizing *only bills in the chamber of origin*. The inferred minimal sponsorship *mean* tends to be higher in smaller chambers but also in states with longer sessions, such as New York and California. The median senate has a minimum per member sponsorship rate of 18.1, and the median house rate is 10.9.

Given the above description, a reasonable estimate of an agenda profile for a legislator might be portrayed as follows:

Proposals in Order of Value

a	b	c	d	e	f	g	h	
P	P	P	P	P	P	P	P	Most Preferred Outcome
P	P	P	P	P	P	P	D	Second Preferred Outcome
P	P	P	P	P	P	D	P	Third Preferred Outcome
								•
								•
								•
D	D	D	D	D	D	D	D	Least Preferred Outcome

P = PASS
D = DEFEAT

The legislator in this example has eight agenda items and his most preferred outcome is that they all pass. Short of that, he prefers that all pass but the last item, and so on. It is expected that most legislators have personal agenda profiles of this sort, loaded with "P's" at the top and left. If we couple this picture with the great number of bills introduced in the modern American legislature, it seems fair to assume that an efficient agenda processing system is in high demand, and that those rank-and-file members with a sizeable agenda have the greatest need for an accommodating committee structure.

The Committee Assignment Process

Committee assignments are crucial because most legislators have an agenda that will be facilitated if they receive their most preferred positions. Perhaps the most complete treatment of the committee assignment process in Congress was developed by Shepsle (1978; also see Rohde and Shepsle, 1973), who fashioned the phrase, "interest–advocacy–accommodation syndrome." In a multisession examination of legislators' backgrounds, requests, and assignments, Shepsle was able to show that members' requests reflected their personal background, training, and experience, and the makeup of their constituency. Furthermore, the leaders (or the committee making the assignment) took into account these factors and made every attempt to accommodate members' requests. To maximize accommodation for their requests, most members actively seek supporters among their state delegation, the appropriate committee personnel, and lobbies. All of this process occurs within the generous confines of the "seniority system."

In the American states, where seniority norms are much less a factor, *accommodation* would appear to be the rule. The chamber officers and party leaders have the individual or shared authority to make standing committee and chair appointments in almost every chamber (See Council of State Governments, 1981, p. 115). In a national survey (1981), legislators from each chamber were asked to respond to the question:

> "How pleased have you been with your committee/subcommittee assignments?"

The three response categories yielded the following frequencies:

1. "Pleased" 1,657 (83.5%)
2. "Neither Pleased nor Displeased" 282 (14.2%)
3. "Displeased" 46 (2.3%)

Majority and minority party legislators alike are pleased with their standing committee assignments. On a scale of 1 to 3 as above, the two groups average 1.15 (N=1290) and 1.26 (N=695) respectively. When five out of six legislators are "pleased" with their committee assignments (and only one out of forty "displeased"), it is pretty good evidence that the leaders are attempting to accommodate them. Satisfaction is not confined to experienced members. Over 80 percent of members in their first or second year of service indicated they were pleased with their assignments. Finally, a majority of members in every chamber (N=99) indicated that they were "pleased" with their assignments.

Note that the above survey item does not ask legislators whether they were pleased with their experience on the committees, or with the outcomes, but only whether they were pleased with their "assignments." It follows then, assuming truthfulness, that they were accommodated by the leadership. It is possible, of course, that legislators tempered their committee assignment requests to match their expectations

Table 2.2 Tendency of Legislators to Sponsor Bills That Are
Assigned to Their Own Committees

	% **Assigned to** **Own Committees**	**Expected** %
Indiana		
House	31%	9%
Senate	45%	27%
Missouri		
House	32%	12%
Senate	46%	20%

The "expected" percent is simply the average number of committee assignments divided by the
number of committees.

of success in receiving those assignments. The survey measure of committee assignment satisfaction does not distinguish between requests and true preferences.

Accommodation of members' committee interests in the assignment phase has a number of important implications. First, *members are able to sort themselves out according to natural diversities of interest.* For Congress, at least, this means a quite heterogeneous assortment of requests (Shepsle, 1978, p. 47), and there is little reason to suspect the states are much different. Basically, there will be an abundance of requests for a small number of powerful standing committees, almost always including those dealing with appropriations, taxation, or budgeting; but beyond the prime committees, interests will be scattered, suited to personal background and constituency makeup.

A second implication is that *members are more likely to be in a position to promote important parts of their agenda.* If we assume that members will have an agenda that corresponds to their personal or constituency interests, and that the standing committee assignments will correspond also, then we would expect that members would be situated on committees to promote their agenda—on the "inside" rather than the outside. We should expect, for example, that members would sponsor legislative measures that go disproportionately to the committees on which they serve. This latter point seems simple enough, but the published literature does not offer us any enlightenment.

An examination of both chambers of Indiana and Missouri can serve as an early confirmation. As illustrated in Table 2.2, the members do in fact sponsor bills that go much more often than chance would allow to the committees on which they serve. For example, if committee assignment made no difference, Indiana House members would see in committee only about 9 percent of the legislation they personally sponsored. In fact they see 31 percent of such legislation come to their own committees. The difference is consistent for all four chambers of the two states.

The data in Table 2.2 do not establish cause and effect. It is entirely possible that the pattern results because members of a committee are approached more often by lobbyists who expect their bills to be assigned to the members' committee. The truth probably should include both explanations. Legislators and lobbyists alike realize the importance of seeking out a base of support in standing committees. Perception on this matter is sharpened by entertaining the opposite case. That is, if members sponsored less than expected proportions of bills assigned to their own committees, then we might infer that they were dissatisfied with their committee assignments—that their interests in fact lie elsewhere.

Legislators have individual agendas, and as a group they have heterogeneous interests. Such heterogeneity is reflected in their agendas and in their standing committee assignment requests. Because members' requests are likely to be accommodated, the proposals that they sponsor or author are likely to appear in the committees on which they serve. These proposals also are likely to be among those they consider most salient. Thus we would expect that *members will prefer most to win on issues assigned to their own committees*. If this is the case, what further action appears rational?

One possible consequence is that members will decide that the standing committees should have their way. Nonmembers will approve committee members' recommendations if it can be assumed that those committee members will reciprocate on later proposals. This amounts to a kind of cooperative, nonzero-sum game. In its extreme form, members would prefer to win on their committee bills more than on all other bills taken together. Such feelings may be common in many legislatures among members of important committees—Ways and Means, for example, or Appropriations. Conversely, we would expect that other members would be less generous toward committees of such overriding importance.

Accommodation in the committee assignment process can lead also to a structural change in the size of committees. While members' requests for committee assignments will be diverse in nature, it is inevitable *that some committees will be more popular than others and that there will be pressure to enlarge the most popular committees*. This tendency has been documented, for example, for the U.S. House of Representatives (Westefield, 1974). Enlarging the popular committees will increase the number of committee assignments per member unless offsetting reductions are made in other committees. Table 2.3 illustrates the pattern for 101 U.S. chambers by providing the mean standing committee size, the standard deviation, and the name and size of the largest committee in each chamber.

As may be observed, only a few chambers in 1981 utilized a uniform committee size (i.e., standard deviation = 0), although several chambers made only one or two exceptions. Exceptions are made most often for committees dealing with appropriations and finance. Likewise, the largest committee in each chamber is usually a committee that directly influences the public purse. The popularity of such committees is well documented for Congress, and while broad-based evidence on transfers and requests is yet not available for states, few seasoned observers would expect contrary patterns. The present data illustrating larger memberships for such committees offers confirmation.

Structural accommodation of the kind described above allows members to sort themselves out in a manner more commensurate with their interests. As a consequence, the notion of reciprocity among committees makes more sense. The so-called important committees have larger memberships, and thus there will be more members who would find the notion of committee rule and reciprocity desirable.

Is there a final payoff in this system of accommodation? That is, do members of committees experience greater success with their legislation when in fact it is assigned to their own committees? Are such proposals enacted more often than those that do not have internal committee sponsors? It seems obvious that bills with internal sponsors would have a better chance of moving forward, but does the final payoff to members justify the effort? Table 2.4 illustrates that in all four chambers of the two test states, Indiana and Missouri, bills sponsored by members on the committee to which they are assigned have greater success.

The data in Table 2.4 are specified to answer the kind of question a legislator might ask: "How much better are my chances of getting bills approved if they are sent to my own committees?" As can be seen, chances of committee approval are approximately 55 to 60 percent in the senates and nearly 50 percent in the house chambers when the member is an internal sponsor. If the member is not an internal sponsor, the committee approval rate drops off from 12 to 19 percent. The advantage of internal sponsorship carries through to enactment.

Table 2.3 Average Committee Size and Standard Deviation by Chamber (1981)

	House Chamber			Senate Chamber		
State	$\bar{X}$	s	Largest Committee	$\bar{X}$	s	Largest Committee
Alabama	14.85	1.70	*	11.58	3.57	Finance & Tax (19)
Alaska	7.44	2.27	Fin. Resources (11)	5.44	.84	Fin. Resources (7)
Arizona	14.75	.97	*	9.45	1.44	Approp (14)
Arkansas	20.00	0.00	*	7.00	0.00	*
California	11.68	3.79	Ways & Means (23)	9.00	2.75	Finance (15)
Colorado	10.18	.58	Finance (12)	8.70	1.79	Approp (14)
Connecticut	21.11	7.90	(J) Approp (43)	21.11	7.90	(J) Approp (43)
Delaware	5.22	.42	Approp, Rev (6)	5.83	.76	*
Florida	17.61	6.00	Rules (35)	10.60	4.72	Approp (23)
Georgia	20.46	9.32	Approp (48)	8.59	5.38	Approp (21)
Hawaii	14.66	1.49	*	7.00	2.23	Ways & Means (11)
Idaho	13.50	3.84	Resources (19)	9.00	.32	Finance (10)
Illinois	16.75	3.22	*	12.71	2.99	Elec & Reapp. (19)
Indiana	11.52	2.30	Ways & Means (22)	9.87	1.90	Finance (16)
Iowa	21.80	3.75	Ways & Means (33)	11.13	3.07	Approp (19)
Kansas	19.23	2.46	Ways & Means (23)	10.22	1.36	*
Kentucky	17.36	1.29	Agri & Nat Res (22)	8.07	.96	*
Louisiana	15.73	2.02	*	7.27	.68	Revenue, Fin (9)
Maine	13.00	0.00	*	13.00	0.00	*
Maryland	23.50	.50	*	10.28	3.57	Exec Nominations (18)
Massachusetts	17.43	1.35	Rules (26)	16.52	2.44	*
Michigan	11.39	3.53	Approp (18)	5.80	2.04	Approp (13)

State						
Nebraska				7.78	.56	Approp (9)
Nevada	9.92	1.49	Ways & Means (13)	6.67	.47	*
New Hampshire	20.48	4.09	Legis Admin (27)	5.07	1.28	Finance (9)
New Jersey	7.33	1.85	Rev & Approp (14)	5.92	2.20	Judiciary (12)
New Mexico	11.46	2.73	Approp, Rev. (17)	11.86	4.05	Finance (21)
New York	19.96	4.81	Rules (34)	12.48	2.87	Finance (24)
North Carolina	18.16	11.88	Approp (65)	12.58	6.07	Approp, Redist (28)
North Dakota	15.91	1.08	Approp (19)	7.64	2.01	Approp (14)
Ohio	13.16	4.00	Fin & Approp (26)	9.10	.57	Finance (11)
Oklahoma	15.33	6.38	Approp, Rules (30)	15.58	.64	Exec Nominations (17)
Oregon	7.88	.97	*	6.78	1.36	Gov Operations (11)
Pennsylvania	23.30	3.18	Approp (32)	10.78	2.44	Approp (20)
Rhode Island	12.77	3.59	*	12.00	2.85	Labor (16)
South Carolina	19.57	3.58	W & M, Judic (25)	18.00	0.00	*
South Dakota	12.55	1.88	Agri & Nat Res (15)	8.00	1.13	Approp (10)
Tennessee	17.16	6.27	Finance (28)	9.88	2.51	Judiciary (17)
Texas	11.22	2.87	Approp (21)	10.33	1.89	Fin, State Aff (13)
Utah	12.62	3.53	Joint Approp Subc	8.41	3.89	Joint Approp Subc
Vermont	9.75	1.39	*	5.92	.64	Approp, Fin (7)
Virginia	18.82	2.12	*	15.00	0.00	*
Washington	15.00	3.68	Transportation (23)	10.19	2.98	Ways & Means (17)
West Virginia	23.92	3.59	*	12.12	3.10	Finance (18)
Wisconsin	10.97	2.62	*	6.33	2.60	Joint Finance (14)
Wyoming	9.09	1.08	*	5.00	0.00	*
U.S. Congress	34.76	10.43	Approp (54)	17.67	4.00	Approp (29)

*Three or more committees were of maximum size.

Table 2.4 Successful Sponsorships: Percent Leading to Committee
Approval or Enactment

	Sponsorships in Own Committees	**Other Sponsorships**
Indiana House	N = 343	N = 750
Success in Committee	46.7% (160)	27.9% (209)
Successful Enactment	23.3% (80)	13.9% (104)
Indiana Senate	N = 333	N = 405
Success in Committee	54.7% (182)	40.2% (163)
Successful Enactment	40.5% (135)	26.9% (109)
Missouri House	N = 315	N = 684
Success in Committee	48.9% (154)	36.3% (248)
Successful Enactment	11.7% (37)	5.3% (36)
Missouri Senate	N = 235	N = 259
Success in Committee	60.1% (143)	44.8% (116)
Successful Enactment	21.7% (51)	14.3% (37)

Number of cases given within parentheses. Data are derived from the official Indexes of the
Journals of each state. Note that the above figures refer to the number of sponsorships (one or two
named sponsors for each bill) and not the number of bills.

Is internal committee sponsorship an advantage even after bills
leave the original committee? In Indiana, the differences are slight. In
the Indiana House, one-half of the bills approved by committee are enacted, showing no delayed effect of internal committee sponsorship. In
the Indiana Senate, internally sponsored bills fare somewhat better
(74% to 67%). In Missouri, the internal sponsorships yield a slight advantage in the Senate (36 to 31%), and in the House a substantial advantage (24 to 15%). In sum, it appears that most of the advantage is gained
in the original committee decision making. Smaller increments in the
success differential later in the process may be due to the possibility that
"smart" or better legislation will tend to have internal committee
sponsors.

Jurisdictions and the Separability of Issues

The varied origins of standing committee jurisdiction defy a complete
listing, but in general it seems that most committees are formed to correspond to executive functions and agencies, or to capture important
clusters of activities in need of regulation and/or subsidy. No doubt
these are important considerations, but to divide up the subject matter is

to impose a set of values about what makes sense in the formulation of policy. Such values may be preimposed by constitution or statute, or they may be subject to the whims of legislative leaders at the beginning of each legislative session. The internal functioning of the legislature is as important as its relationship to its environment.

Why are standing committees not simply numbered rather than named, and the bills assigned randomly as they appear? Members would then serve on committees of about equal importance, and the workload of each committee would be about the same. Of course one important defect in this scheme would be lack of subject-matter expertise. Not only would members be unable to choose committees for which they had the best qualifications, but they would also miss the specialized training of specialized committees. Many observers would reject the scheme for these reasons alone.

Another important defect would result from the assignment of related proposals to different committees. A bicameral system is prone to duplication of effort as it is, but if the duplication were rampant within chambers, the cost effectiveness of the system might be unbearable. In practice, related bills normally are assigned to the same committee. Subject-matter designations, as employed by legislatures, provide a way of placing related legislation in the same hands. A more sophisticated way of describing this process is to say that legislation involving *inseparable preferences* would be placed in the same committee.

Committee jurisdictions may be divided in a number of ways, and one way is to keep in mind the separability or inseparability of issues. Issues with separable preferences can go to different committees, because their outcomes seem unrelated. Issues with inseparable preferences can go to the same committee to encourage resolution at the committee level rather than on the floor. *The standing committees make it possible for members to work with separable subsets of inseparable preferences.*

If proposals within a standing committee do exhibit separable preferences, they can be assigned to appropriate subcommittees. When proposals of different committees reach the floor of the chamber, they will tend to be characterized by separable preferences. *If the preferences are separable, the order in which proposals from different standing committees appear on the floor will not influence member preferences, and sophisticated voting across separate bills will be unnecessary.* For any given proposal, of course, amendments can complicate matters. It is also possible that vote trading can tie together otherwise separable issues.

Much of the reciprocity that may develop among standing committees may relate to the defeat of legislation. In other words, members seldom challenge either the negative vote of the committee or its decision to sit on the legislation. But even for legislation that reaches the floor, members may reason that since it is unrelated to their most salient issues, the other committees should be allowed to have their way.

The separability argument can be carried too far. It is apparent that many proposals border on the jurisdictions of two or more committees and that such proposals will present special problems if the committees disagree. Governments must work also with a finite budget, and all legislation that affects revenues or appropriations will affect that budget. In a strict logical sense, all proposals affecting the budget are related and would seem to stimulate inseparable preferences. Most legislatures illustrate recognition of this interrelatedness by forming committees to oversee fiscal matters. Typically, for example, all matters that involve funding or a funding change must be sent to an appropriations committee. Congress separates authorization and appropriation decisions so that there are many authorization committees but only one appropriations committee in each chamber. Many states utilize a second committee referral rule to accomplish the same. In Congress and in many state chambers the appropriations process has become decentralized through the use of subcommittees. In such cases it is common to find the creation of either a budget committee or an "executive" subcommittee in order to consider overall fiscal policy. In several states (Arkansas, Colorado, Delaware, South Dakota, Utah, Wisconsin, and Wyoming) the two chambers consolidate the financing function through a "joint" finance committee, while allowing other functions to be carried out in the traditional bicameral two-stage process.

The lower chamber of the state of Indiana offers an example of a strong ways and means committee. It receives directly or by recommittal almost all tax and appropriation measures. The "subject index" of the 1981 session's *Index to House and Senate Journals* lists bills according to topic. The committee received:

a. All eight bills affecting local adjusted gross income taxes.

b. All five bills affecting state adjusted income taxes (excludes one reorganization bill).

c. Twenty-seven of thirty bills allowing credits or exemptions to state adjusted gross income taxes. The committee was by-passed on one energy credit, one environmental credit, and one election campaign fund credit, only one of which passed the chamber.

d. Forty-two of the forty-four bills affecting property taxes (excludes two tax neutral bills).

e. All five of the major budget bills.

Clearance through the Ways and Means Committee is seldom breached, since it is the committee charged with resolving revenue-expenditure imbalances. Its twenty-two members thus deal with the inseparabilities of state revenue and appropriation measures.

The sorting of issues into separable subsets may be illustrated by examining a particular subject such as "alcoholic beverages." In 1981, members of the Indiana House introduced nineteen bills on this subject. Two affected excise taxes and were sent directly to the Ways and Means Committee. Three involved the regulation of crimes and offenses and were sent directly to the Committee on Courts and Criminal Procedure. The remaining fourteen were proposals affecting licensing and permits and were sent to the Committee on Public Policy & Veterans Affairs. The latter committee obviously had more than one subject to manage, but it could divide into subcommittees if the chairman of the committee felt that the agenda required it.

To take another example, there were nineteen proposals that fall under the heading of "solid waste." Seven of these bills affected taxes, financing methods, or state expenditures and were referred to the Ways and Means Committee. Another seven bills went to the Committee on Environmental Affairs. These bills affected hazardous waste treatment, recycling programs, and water pollution control. Each of the remaining five bills landed in a different committee: one regulating garbage refuse trucks was assigned to the Committee on Roads and Transportation; a second affecting the authority of the City of Indianapolis was assigned to the Committee on Urban Affairs; a third reestablishing a solid waste management study commission was sent to the Committee on Energy; a fourth affecting allowable per diem payments to regional water and solid waste boards was given to the Committee on County and Township; and a final bill affecting the authority of solid waste districts to issue bonds found its way to the Committee on Public Policy and Veterans Affairs. In sum, most assignments make sense in light of the separable versus inseparable distinction, but at times other factors are surely at work. Legislators sometimes insist on an assignment of a personal bill to their own committee, even if it more appropriately belongs elsewhere. Legislative leaders are not above placing bills in committees where they feel the outcome will be more to their liking. And no doubt mistakes are made.

If legislators are able to create a standing committee system that divides the subject matter into separate bundles of issues, so that preferences of individuals are separable for proposals in different committees, then the potential for reciprocity among committees is enhanced. It is less likely to break down as the issues on the floor arise. As we noted above, if proposals on the floor exhibit separable preferences, the order in which they appear is not a factor, and sophisticated voting is not helpful. The proposals will be advanced according to committee recommendations, unencumbered by policy ties to the proposals of other committees. Where this advancement does not occur, we would expect to find that there had been severe disagreement within the originating committee, and that such disagreement had been passed on to a floor fight. We might speculate that such a situation would stimulate logrolling for floor supremacy and that the chamber leadership would have an active role in determining the outcome.

The traditional view is that committees and subcommittees serve as power bases for the chairs, allowing those in alliance with the majority party leaders to control particular areas of policy. Only in Congress, where seniority is very important, would we be likely to see the alliances break down. This analysis shows, however, that the internal forces for decentralized agenda setting in American legislatures are rooted in a logic of individual choice—that is, in individual pursuit of approval for legislative proposals.

The pieces of the puzzle fit. Members receive committee assignments in accordance with their preferences. They are likely to sponsor legislation assigned to their own committees. Legislative proposals assigned to the sponsor's committee are more likely to survive the committee and more likely to be enacted. These observations have been supported by direct evidence. In addition, we might infer that members' interests can be enhanced through norms of reciprocity among committees, and that reciprocity itself is enhanced when committees deal with "separate" bundles of issues.

While tendencies toward decentralization are very strong in U.S. legislatures, the fifty states exhibit ample variety in this regard. The next chapter (chapter 3) contains an analysis of the relative importance of committee and party influence in each state. The next logical question—Does decentralization pay dividends?—is the subject of chapter 4.

3

Party Leadership, Party Caucuses, and Standing Committees: Why Committee Outcomes Are Preferred in the United States

The pressures for action in a legislative setting may create a number of tensions. Many scholars, for example, see a natural tension between the party officers and the committee chieftains (e.g., Huitt, 1961; Dodd and Oppenheimer, 1977, 21–53; Rosenthal, 1974, 57–58; Uslaner and Weber, 1977, 74–105). The seniority system no doubt heightens this tension in the U.S. Congress. For the states at least, the tensions arise more amorphously from inherent conflicts among demands for action, the scarcity of time and resources, and leadership versus rank-and-file intentions. How can the legislative party leaders resolve these tensions and conflicts?

Party Leadership versus Committee Leadership

One time-honored approach places emphasis on party leadership and discipline. The majority party leaders attempt to build a winning party coalition, both in an active caucus and by assigning key members to important chair positions and committees. The party leadership's agenda takes precedence at every step, in committees, in caucus, and on the floor. Members are rewarded or punished in accordance with their degree of support for "leadership" or "party" positions. The committees exist primarily to serve the agenda-processing needs of the majority party leadership (as assumed in the Liebowitz-Tollison thesis discussed in the previous chapter). In other words, in-depth committee consideration allows for easier ratification when bills reach the floor of the chamber.

In a second, contrasting type of management, the leadership is not in a position (or does not choose) to develop or enforce a wide range of party policies. Instead it attempts to build up credits that will eventually aid the passage of its agenda. It does this in part by honoring as many members' requests for chair appointments and committee assignments as possible. By the beginning of the sessions, the party leaders (usually the speaker or majority leader, but also a "committee on committees" in many cases) pass out the chairmanship and assignment favors. The committees then act autonomously, and the chairs of committees pretty much determine the committee agenda. The party leaders must take their chances and rely upon the good will of the committee members for support on those items that head their leadership agenda.

In reality we would expect most legislative systems to have less than extreme orientations, neither strictly centralized into a leadership agenda, nor strictly decentralized into a committee agenda. One possibility, for example, is that the leadership will have a fairly short agenda and that, upon its likely accomplishment, other noncontradictory demands will be accommodated. Another possibility is that there will be an implicit understanding of reciprocation. The party leaders will get their way on major party issues relating to, say, fiscal policy, but the committees will get their way on everything else. In other states there may be a continuous interplay between the leadership, the caucus, and the committees.

There is reason to speculate, however, that in recent years the trend has been toward committee-oriented decision making. The pressures created by the increased volume of legislation (Rosenthal and Forth, 1978), the often cited decline of party organization in campaign management (e.g., Agranoff, 1972), and the increase in subcommittee importance or use, all suggest that the parties in legislatures may be losing ground to the committees. The purpose of this chapter is to examine present patterns of decision making in U.S. state legislatures, where less is known, and to assess three factors related to this more general concern:

1. Party leadership accommodation and committee autonomy.
2. Membership views of where "significant" decisions are made.
3. Membership satisfaction with party caucus and standing committee decisions.

Accommodation and Autonomy

The mere existence of standing committees to some extent foretells the expansion of agenda setting to those other than the elected party leadership. Nevertheless, it is still possible that accommodation in the committee assignment process, as discussed in the last chapter, does not lead to very much autonomy at the committee level. Nationwide survey evidence, however, demonstrates that the agenda-setting power of the standing committee chairman is widely recognized. Four out of five respondents from a survey of approximately two thousand state legislators indicate that:

> "A chairman usually has almost full control over the committee agenda."

In only two of ninety-nine chambers (the Massachusetts House and the South Carolina Senate) did more than half the respondents indicate that the chair did not have full control of the agenda. In only two additional states (Illinois and Tennessee) did more than one-third in both chambers indicate that the chair had less than full control of the agenda. In other words, chair domination of the agenda is nearly universal—recognized by a substantial majority of respondents in almost every chamber.

A great many committees also employ subcommittees. More than two-thirds of the respondents in the survey indicated that

> "Subcommittees are used on a regular basis in many committees"

or that

> "Subcommittees are an official part of my chamber rules and at least some committees are required to use them."

While in most states (if not all states) we would not expect the degree of subcommittee autonomy that has been reported for Congress, the use of subcommittees does tend to disperse even further the power of agenda setting. Subcommittee chairs will have some control over the order in which issues are considered, and they may possibly be in a position to keep proposals from active consideration.

The fact that the chairs determine the agenda within the standing committees does not mean that they necessarily deviate from the wishes of the elected party leaders. Nor does it mean necessarily that they get their way on those issues that they bring before the committee. But in either case it seems clear that substantial decision-making authority is delegated to the committees. The memberships of committees are developed in the first instance on a cooperative bipartisan basis, at least to the extent of allowing even most minority party members to receive desirable committee assignments.

When proposals are sent to standing committees, business is likely to be conducted with less partisanship than on the floor of the chamber, and to some extent this factor may undermine party discipline or leadership positions on issues. In studies of several national legislatures (the U.S., Britain, Canada, India, Italy, West Germany, the Philippines, and Chile), for example, it has been observed that partisanship is less a factor in committee decision making than in full chamber decision making (Lees, et al., 1979, p. 424). The same phenomenon occurs in state legislatures. Legislators were questioned:

"Where would you say partisanship is most evident in your chamber?"

The responses distributed as follows (N > 2000):

During floor proceedings	73.5%
During committee proceedings	14.3%
During subcommittee proceedings	1.7%
Not evident in my chamber	10.5%

Importantly, the committee system can encourage nonpartisan or bipartisan decision making.

None of the above is to deny that partisanship plays an important role. The standing committee chairs are appointed from the majority party (with few exceptions), and the majority party will have a majority in every committee. Minority party members are going to be less satisfied than majority members with committee decisions. There are other factors, however, that may modify the extent of partisanship. For example, between one-third and two-thirds of the states are normally under divided control. If a stalemate is to be avoided, the leaders may need to seek bipartisan cooperation.

The principal factor that reduces partisanship, however, is probably the task orientation of the smaller group. As a problem solving unit, partisanship is less often a helpful way of disposing of an issue or proposal. Hamm has shown, for example, that legislators frequently do change their votes between the committee and floor actions on a measure, even when the bill has not been amended. These changes tend to be in the direction of partisan voting (Hamm, 1982). One reason a legislator may change votes between the committee and floor stages is that the caucus or leadership of the party may intervene. The legislator may feel subsequently that it is necessary to support the "party" when the proposal comes to a final vote.

Importance of Leadership, Caucus, and Committee Decisions

Previous evidence suggests that leaders do what they can to accommodate rank-and-file members in the committee assignment process. There is still the question, however, of whether the committees really make important decisions. In the internal organization of the chamber it is possible that much of the decision-making power rests in the hands of the majority party leadership and the majority party caucus. The committees may be left with little more than the details, or they may serve simply as sounding boards for the leadership. One way to examine this question is to evaluate the perceptions of the legislative participants. Legislators were asked:

> "In your legislature where would you say the most significant decisions are made?"

The choices available were (See Appendix 9.1):

1. Office of Presiding Officers or Majority Leaders
2. Regular Committee Meetings
3. Party Caucus
4. In Governor's Office
5. On the Floor
6. In Policy Committee

7. In Subcommittees
8. Pre-legislative Session
9. Other

In this section we need to assess the responses only to the first three choices. They are in fact the most often selected and they do focus upon the party and committee responsibilities. In the survey, legislators were asked to select the top three decision-making loci, in rank order if possible. For the purposes of this particular analysis, the judgments are accumulated on a chamber by chamber basis. A decision "arena" is highlighted only when at least 50 percent of majority party respondents selected it as one of the three principal centers of important decision making. To rule out the possibility of confusion of minority with majority party organization, only responses of majority party members will be utilized.

The 50 percent criterion was met by the "party caucus" item in 50 of the 99 chambers. The chamber party "leadership" response met the criterion in 67 chambers, and the "regular committee meetings" were seen as important by at least half the majority party respondents in 81 chambers. We would expect that the influence of legislative *party* organization would be most prevalent in those states in which members see significant decisions made by the party leadership, the party caucus, or both.

In Figure 3.1 the states and chambers are grouped according to the significance of the three decision-making centers. Several important features of the classification emerge:

1. At the top left are those chambers in which the committees are dominant and no appreciable party influence is apparent. These fifteen chambers are mostly in states with a tradition of one-party dominance (or *no* parties, as in Nebraska).

2. A second group of twenty-nine chambers illustrates the importance of committee and party leadership decision making, but not the party caucus. Here again, these chambers are almost entirely in states with either a dominant party or a lopsided party advantage in the legislative session of that year (1981). In such states the party leadership does not work through the caucus—which may be large and unwieldy if not superfluous—but through the committees and committee chairs.

3. In contrast to the committee-oriented chambers are the chambers that appear to be principally party-oriented, especially those in

which both the caucus and leadership are seen as important. In the latter group are primarily those chambers from states with long traditions of party competition and government—New York, Pennsylvania, New Jersey, Indiana, Illinois, Connecticut, and so forth. In such chambers the leadership is more likely to work consistently through the caucus. The committees are less important. Only eighteen of the ninety-nine chambers are in this group, and two-thirds of this number are the smaller state senates. In the larger house chambers, the leadership apparently relies more often upon committee management of legislation.

4. Somewhat more complex are the twenty-one chambers in which all three decision-making loci are seen as important. Two-thirds of these chambers are house chambers. We may surmise that in these chambers the leadership exerts its influence through, and works with, both the party caucus and the standing committees, but that the caucus and committees have the ability to act autonomously from time to time. The states in this group tend to have two competitive parties, each having a sizeable share of the seats.

5. In the final group are the chambers in which the committees and majority caucuses are seen as important decision-making centers, but the leadership is not so seen in any independent sense. Most of these chambers have relatively few members and can operate more informally than could more numerous memberships. The party leadership may blend inconspicuously into the party caucus proceedings, wherein perhaps committee chairs vociferously announce their intentions. It is evident that the major industrial states do not have chambers in this category. The chambers in contrast represent more rural states, where perhaps the legislative environment encourages a less demanding leadership. It is also possible that the governor in some states displaces the role of the internal party leadership, but additional evidence did not support this explanation.

In sum, the balance of committee or party oriented decision making varies considerably among the states. The majority caucus is passive in most southern states as well as in several other states with a single dominant party. In many of these same states, however, the party leadership is very active and engages in important decision making. We can speculate that in such cases the leadership exercises control, to the extent that it can, through the committee system, but that the relationship is reciprocal. In a few states both the caucus and the committees are important decision-making centers, and an active leadership must deal with both.

Fig. 3.1 Classification of State Chambers According to Importance
of Party and Committee Decision Making (Criterion:
50% of majority party respondents selected survey item)

COMMITTEES	LEADERSHIP	CAUCUS
(15)	(5)	(1)
Arkansas (H,S)	Alaska (S)	Michigan (S)
Georgia (S)	Florida (H)	
Hawaii (S)	Illinois (H)	
Louisiana (H,S)	Mass. (S)	
Kentucky (S)	Rhode Island (S)	
Maryland (H,S)		
Nebraska		
Nevada (H)		
Oregon (H,S)		
S. Carolina (H,S)		

LEADERSHIP
↕
COMMITTEES

(29)

Alabama (H,S) Florida (S)
Georgia (H) Hawaii (H)
Maine (H) Massachusetts (H)
Michigan (H) Mississippi (H,S)
Missouri (H,S) Nevada (S)
New Hampshire (H,S) N.M. (H,S)
North Carolina (H,S) Ohio (H)
Rhode Island (H) Tenn. (H,S)
Texas (H,S) Vermont (H)
Virginia (H,S) W. Virginia (H)

LEADERSHIP
↕
CAUCUS

(12)

California (H,S)
Connecticut (H)
Illinois (S)
Indiana (S)
Iowa (H)
New Jersey (H,S)
New York (S)
Ohio (S)
Oklahoma (S)
Pennsylvania (S)

LEADERSHIP
COMMITTEES ← → CAUCUS

(21)

Arizona (H,S) Colorado (H) Connecticut (S)
Delaware (H) Idaho (H) Indiana (H) Iowa (S)
Kansas (H,S) Minnesota (H,S) Montana (H)
New York (H) North Dakota (H) Oklahoma (H)
Pennsylvania (H) Utah (H) Washington, (H,S)
West Virginia (S)

COMMITTEES ← → CAUCUS

(16)

Alaska (H) Colorado (S) Delaware (S) Idaho (S)
Kentucky (H) Maine (S) Montana (H) N. Dakota (S)
S. Dakota (H,S) Utah (S) Vermont (S) Wisconsin (H,S)
Wyoming (H,S)

Figure 3.1 illustrates one way to interpret the data. When multiple centers of decision making are seen as important in a chamber, the influence patterns are reciprocal and not reflective of dominant-submissive relationships.

Figure 3.1 is constructed from selected data, the responses of majority party members only, and the consensus responses (50% agreement) when aggregated at the chamber level. A somewhat different approach can be taken by examining three alternative dependent variables:

1. The percent of majority party respondents from each chamber who indicate that significant decisions are made by the *party caucus*. (Y_1)

2. The percent in each chamber who indicate that significant decisions are made by the *party leadership*. (Y_2)

3. The percent in each chamber who indicate that significant decisions are made by regular *committees*. (Y_3)

We might assume that the perceptions that elicit these responses are influenced by actual decision-making activity in the chambers, not necessarily in specific cases but in the statistical aggregate. In turn, the type of decision making that legislators adopt may be influenced by specific structural conditions. The two structural features of legislatures that appear to have an impact on the type of legislative decision making that the chambers adopt are:

1. The share of the seats held by the majority party (%MAJ)

2. The number of members in the chamber (CHSIZE)

For each dependent variable, Y_1, Y_2, and Y_3, the OLS model

$$Y_i = a + b_1 (\%MAJ) + b_2 (CHSIZE) + e_i \qquad 3.1$$

may be employed to test for whether there is a statistically discernible impact upon perceptions of where significant decisions are made. An asterisk is inserted in Table 3.1 to indicate which of these terms had a significant t value ($t > 2.0$) in each of the three applications.

The results suggest that the party *caucuses* are most important in small chambers with evenly matched parties. They are least important in large chambers with a dominant party. The party *leadership* appears to gain significance in larger chambers, but does not fare as well in a dominant party. In such dominant parties the *committees* take on added importance.

To counterbalance the decentralizing effect of committee organiza-

Table 3.1   Influence of Majority Party Advantage and Chamber Size
on Party and Committee Decision Making (*r* values,
N = 98)

	% of Responses Indicating "Significant Decisions" Made by		
	Party Caucus Y_1	Party Leadership Y_2	Regular Committees Y_3
% of Members in Majority Party	−.576*	−.218*	.240*
Chamber Size	−.205*	.262*	.061
R^2	.383	.112	.06

tion, majority leaders may choose to work through a party caucus. The
evidence suggests, however, that they do not do this as often in chambers with large memberships, especially when their party owns a high
proportion of the seats. In large memberships, the caucus setting is
somewhat cumbersome and too time-consuming to process very much
legislation. When one party dominates the seat distribution in the chamber, it dominates also the seat distribution in committees, and no doubt
it is easier for the majority party position to win in committees. As a
consequence, the need for an active party caucus is less. In some cases
the minority party is nonexistent, or nearly so, and thus a majority party
caucus is at best unnecessary.

Ratings of Caucus and Committee Outcomes

The foregoing analysis offers statistical confirmation that legislative
leaders tend to employ caucus meetings when there is some rational expectation of gain—when the caucus will aid in the passage of the
leadership agenda. The caucus seems to be more helpful in smaller
chambers where the proceedings are perhaps less cumbersome, and in
those parties with a small plurality where committee decisions are more
likely to run contrary to leadership preferences. To examine caucus and
committee decision making in greater depth, we can evaluate only those
fifty chambers (appearing in Figure 3.1) with an "important" majority
party caucus.

In the national survey, state legislators were asked to respond to two related items:

1. How *satisfied* were you with those *bills that were passed or recommended favorably* by the following units of your legislature?

2. How *satisfied* were you with the decisions *not to consider, recommend unfavorably, or defeat bills* by the following units?

The organizational units in question were:

- Committee A (Named earlier by respondent, respondent is a member)
- Committee B (Named earlier by respondent, respondent is a member)
- In General, My Committees (If respondent has more than two)
- The Other Committees of the Chamber
- My Party Caucus
- My Chamber as a Whole

Each respondent was asked to indicate his or her "degree of satisfaction" by selecting one of five responses, "very high," "high," "medium," "low," and "very low," which were displayed in a Likert-type format for each of the above named organizational units. The response categories were given numeric scores of one through five.

The two organizational units of concern here are "My Party Caucus" and "In General, My Committees." Legislator responses to these two items can serve as their satisfaction ratings of the decisions made by each unit. For purposes of illustration, each of the fifty selected chambers may be assessed by subtracting the mean committee satisfaction rating from the mean majority party caucus satisfaction rating. The results of the calculations for decisions to *pass* legislation and decisions to *defeat* legislation are presented in Table 3.2. As may be seen, in most cases (71%) majority party legislators register greater satisfaction with their committee decisions. In fewer cases (15%) greater preference for their majority caucus decisions is shown, and in some instances (14%) no difference is recorded.

How are these results to be interpreted? We have isolated those chambers in which the majority party caucus is considered an important decision-making center, yet in most of these same chambers it appears that legislators of the majority party are more satisfied with the deci-

Table 3.2   Satisfaction Ratings: Mean Differences between Party
Caucus and Committees for Fifty Chambers in Which Party
Caucus Is Important.* (Majority Party Responses Only)

| | House | | Senate | |
| | Decisions to | | Decisions to | |
State	Pass	Defeat	Pass	Defeat
Alaska	−.33	−.58		
Arizona	−.33	−.06	−.33	.00
California	−.11	+.11	.00	−.50
Colorado	−.55	−.81	−1.00	−.90
Connecticut	−1.00	−.20	−.42	.00
Delaware	−.50	−.91	−.25	.00
Idaho	−.64	−.46	+.27	−.04
Illinois			.00	.00
Indiana	−.50	−.62	−.11	−.07
Iowa	−.19	−.33	+.29	−.13
Kansas	−.58	−.38	−.08	−.18
Kentucky	−.14	−.23		
Maine			.00	−.33
Michigan			−.67	−1.33
Minnesota	−.31	+.29	−.50	.00
Montana	.00	−.41	−1.00	−.71
New Jersey	−.92	−.15	−.71	−.14
New York	−.04	−.15	+.67	+.67
North Dakota	−.08	+.07	−.29	−.23
Ohio			+.33	−.33
Oklahoma	−.25	−.21	−.80	−.33
Pennsylvania	+.25	.00	+.20	.00
South Dakota	+.04	−.44	−.15	+.04
Utah	−.18	−.10	−.23	−.04
Vermont			−.63	−.33
Washington	−.08	−.32	+.10	+.14
West Virginia			.00	.00
Wisconsin	−.47	−.17	.00	.00
Wyoming	−.94	−.63	−1.11	−1.31

*Satisfaction ratings of decisions to pass and decisions to defeat are utilized. For each chamber the ratings are averaged for those referring to the party caucus and those referring to the committees. The mean committee rating is subtracted from the mean party caucus rating, thus, a negative sign means that the committee decisions were more preferred. These quantities are given to illustrate an overall pattern, and not to indicate exact magnitudes.

sions of committees. The simplest answer to this puzzle is that in committees legislators as a whole have more input into the decisions, and thus it follows that in a random sample survey of this kind, members of the majority party would register greater satisfaction with the committee decisions. The party caucus tends to be a more centralized form of decision making.

Evidence presented earlier, however, suggested that the committee chairs had almost complete control over the agenda. Would not members find this just as frustrating? Some members do, but an examination of the data reveals first, that more than half of the majority party respondents served as a committee chair, and second, that when comparing members who were committee chairs with those who were not, the preference ratings were almost identical. Both groups are more satisfied with committee decisions.

Implicit in the above explanation is the assumption that individual input leads to satisfaction. It is reasonable to expect that because standing committees (and their subcommittees) have fewer members than the majority caucus, the members will have more input into the committee decisions. There is still the possibility, however, that the party caucus will actually improve upon the committee decisions. It seems unlikely that many legislators will see the caucus in this light, though, since the accommodating committee assignment process allows them to sort themselves out into "communities of interest." These communities of interest are able to locate highly preferred policy alternatives, and the alternatives are more likely to be diluted, if changed at all, at the caucus stage. Bills do not reach the caucus for approval, normally, unless they are approved by the committee, and from the perspective of the respective committee members, the caucus is more likely to impose a "different" view, not an improvement.

The above evaluation does not apply to members of the minority party in each chamber. An overall comparison of majority and minority member satisfaction with decisions to pass and decisions to defeat legislation may be accomplished by asking what percent in each group rated:

1. Committee outcomes higher than caucus outcomes.

2. Committee outcomes the same as caucus outcomes.

3. Caucus outcomes higher than committee outcomes.

The results displayed in Table 3.3 illustrate that minority party members do tend to favor their party caucus outcomes. Over 40 percent prefer caucus outcomes, another 30 percent are indifferent, and between 25

Table 3.3   Comparison of Majority and Minority Party Member Preferences for Committee versus Caucus Outcomes

Decision Type		Outcome Preference		
		Committee *(C > P)*	*Indifferent* *(C = P)*	*Caucus* *(P > C)*
Decisions to Pass	Majority	416 42.58%	407 41.66%	154 15.76%
	Minority	162 29.03%	158 28.32%	238 42.65%
Decisions to Defeat	Majority	329 36.15%	451 49.56%	130 14.29%
	Minority	126 24.42%	160 31.01%	230 44.57%

Cases are excluded from this table when legislators did not respond to both questions—as would be appropriate if their chamber party did not have a caucus.

and 30 percent prefer committee outcomes. In contrast, only 15 percent of majority party members prefer caucus outcomes.

Conclusion

The elected leaders in the legislative chambers have a number of important choices to make in the management of legislative business. One of these is the manner in which committee positions are filled. Will the party leaders attempt to build a cohesive winning coalition that rewards primarily members of the coalition? Or will they attempt to accommodate the members of the coalition? Or will they attempt to accommodate the members by passing out as many "favors" as possible at the beginning of the legislative session? The evidence suggests that for committee assignments the latter approach is usually selected. A great majority of members of both parties receive committee assignments they consider desirable. In most cases the leaders also have the flexibility to vary the size of committees and to increase the number of committees. By increasing the membership of the more popular committees and by increasing the number of committee chairmanships, more members are accommodated, and as the party leaders may hope, more members are indebted to them for future support.

Coalition favoritism in state legislative chambers is probably more apparent in the choices to fill committee chair positions. Within the committees, the committee chairs control the agenda. Since the most significant committees, such as appropriations or ways and means, tend to be the busiest and receive the most proposals, the chairs will have ample opportunity to be selective and to enhance the coalition interests. Working in the opposite direction, however, are the decentralizing forces of the standing committee organization. The assignment process allows members to sort themselves out into communities of interest—agriculture, primary and secondary education, health and hospitals, banking, insurance, and so forth. For example, legislators were asked to indicate for two of their committees whether "Members of the committee share a similar perspective to a greater degree than do members of my chamber as a whole." In nearly half the cases, legislators gave a positive response. (This was not a forced choice response of yes or no. Members were asked to check this item if they thought it applied to their experience.)

The style of leadership management is no doubt in part a function of elementary features of chamber and party structure. In many chambers the lack of party competition leads to a lack of party control, thus an increase in party control would depend upon a prior increase in election competition. This "problem" is not a new one, and many observers would no doubt point out that the magnitude of it was perhaps equally great thirty years ago when the southern states had fewer Republican officeholders. Chamber size may be a more recent impediment to party control, due mainly to the enormous increase in bill introduction. With more numerous and diverse demands for action the leaders have found it necessary to rely to a greater extent on the standing committees or committee chairs.

The party caucus is a principal instrument for exercising party control, and it is an important center of decision making in about half the state chambers. In most of these chambers, however, the majority members are more satisfied with their standing committee decisions than with their caucus decisions. It has been suggested that this may be due in part to greater individual input in standing committees and to the tendency to form "communities of interest." These are the forces that can undermine party leadership control, especially if a norm of reciprocity develops among committees that bypasses leadership preferences. Further understanding of these relationships can be achieved perhaps by an in-depth study of fewer states, comparing states in which the party caucus is particularly successful (e.g., Pennsylvania) with those in which it does not succeed so well.

4

Does Decentralized Agenda Setting Pay Dividends?

In legislatures it is important to understand whether the organizations manage the agenda in a centralized or decentralized fashion. Except in Nebraska, centralization means a strong role for the party leadership, perhaps aided by the party caucus which can intervene between committee and floor decisions. Decentralization means that agenda setting is delegated away from the leadership to the standing committees and even to the subcommittees.

The analysis of legislative decision making does not deny the crucial role that the chief executive may have in agenda setting. Active governors and presidents usually get their concerns near the top of the legislative agenda. Various forms of the veto power put the chief executive in a strong position. In evaluating the powers of state governors, for example, Schlesinger (1965) and Dometrius (1979) give substantial weight to the legislative powers of governors. The impact of the chief executive, however, is often exaggerated. The major concerns of the chief executive are usually the major concerns of many if not most legislators. President Carter's energy legislation was no surprise to Congress, and members of Congress promptly dismantled it and constructed their own versions.

Evidence presented earlier has illustrated that members of legislatures do have their individual agendas and that they locate on committees likely to receive such items for consideration. Such a strategy appears to pay dividends to the extent that bills are more likely to emerge from committee when there are internal sponsors and to the extent that such bills are more likely to be enacted into law. Logic suggests that even greater dividends result wben reciprocity among committees is strong. In the extreme, such decentralized agenda setting and reciprocity may extend to the subcommittees. The neatness of these organizational arrangements can break down, of course, if jurisdictional boundaries are messy, or if preferences are inseparable across issues in different committees or subcommittees. Congress has had such problems, for example, in energy and environmental legislation.

In a decentralized committee system, where agenda setting occurs in standing committees and subcommittees and where some degree of reciprocity exists, we might expect that legislation would have a greater chance of success. The chamber passage rate, for example, would tend to be higher in decentralized systems. The empirical question may be stated precisely:

> Does centralization (or decentralization) have a statistically discernable impact upon chamber passage rates?

If centralization does have an impact, to what extent are legislators correspondingly less satisfied with the decisions of the chamber?

The Bill Passage Rate

The magnitude of state legislative agendas is illustrated in Table 4.1, which contains a listing of the number of house and senate bills in each of fifty states, along with the number and percentage that pass each chamber (the figures do not include resolutions or special session legislation). Although a major proportion of the bills introduced are offered in the first instance by lobbyists and representatives of other governmental units, to obtain official standing they must receive the sponsorship of at least one legislator. Furthermore, with modern bill drafting services, legislators themselves are more able to take the initiative. Regardless of the origins of legislation, the fact is that most legislators want to initiate changes in the status quo. The agenda for most legislators is an agenda for change—bills for their district, from their campaign, from supportive interest groups, or for future credit claims on popular positions.

Table 4.1 Number of House and Senate Bills Received by Each State Chamber, 1981, and Final Chamber Action

State	Chamber	# of Chamber Bills	# of Chamber Bills Passed	% Passed	# of Bills from Other Chamber	# of Bills from Other Chamber Passed	% Passed	Total Bills Received	Total Bills Passed	% Passed
Alabama	House	1130	491	.435	253	141	.557	1383	632	.457
	Senate	668	253	.379	491	400	.815	1159	653	.563
Alaska	House	1051	225	.214	378	203	.537	1429	428	.300
	Senate	1037	378	.365	225	157	.698	1262	535	.424
Arizona	House	496	269	.542	213	163	.765	709	432	.609
	Senate	410	213	.520	269	194	.721	679	407	.599
Arkansas	House	1018	681	.669	513	445	.867	1531	1126	.735
	Senate	629	513	.816	681	600	.881	1310	1113	.850
California	House	2303	1267	.550	781	561	.718	3084	1828	.593
	Senate	1281	781	.610	1267	716	.565	2548	1497	.588
Colorado	House	624	313	.502	350	280	.800	974	593	.609
	Senate	522	350	.670	313	255	.815	835	605	.725
Connecticut	House	2410	299	.124	291	270	.928	2701	569	.211
	Senate	1463	291	.199	299	284	.950	1762	575	.326
Delaware	House	486	202	.416	200	138	.690	686	340	.495
	Senate	384	200	.521	202	163	.806	586	363	.619
Florida	House	1193	505	.423	338	229	.678	1531	734	.479
	Senate	1095	338	.309	505	284	.562	1600	622	.389
Georgia	House	1140	667	.585	331	236	.713	1471	903	.613
	Senate	458	331	.723	667	603	.904	1125	934	.830

State	Chamber									
Hawaii	House	1942	274	.141	230	83	2172	.361	357	.164
	Senate	2131	230	.107	274	195	2405	.712	425	.177
Idaho	House	463	303	.654	175	142	638	.811	445	.697
	Senate	238	175	.735	303	220	541	.726	395	.730
Illinois	House	2012	631	.314	674	405	2686	.601	1036	.386
	Senate	1273	674	.529	631	424	1904	.672	1098	.576
Indiana	House	1122	323	.288	186	143	1308	.769	466	.356
	Senate	506	186	.368	323	197	829	.610	383	.462
Iowa	House	878	214	.244	230	129	1108	.561	343	.310
	Senate	579	230	.397	214	130	793	.607	360	.454
Kansas	House	609	264	.433	287	200	896	.697	464	.518
	Senate	483	287	.594	264	187	747	.708	474	.635
Kentucky	House	825	350	.424	220	151	1045	.686	501	.479
	Senate	404	220	.545	350	283	754	.808	503	.667
Louisiana	House	1919	846	.441	508	295	2427	.581	1141	.470
	Senate	1130	508	.450	846	732	1976	.865	1240	.628
Maine	House	1201	468	.390	190	176	1391	.926	644	.463
	Senate	434	190	.438	468	439	902	.938	629	.697
Maryland	House	2019	707	.350	628	372	2647	.592	1079	.408
	Senate	1198	628	.524	707	567	1905	.802	1195	.627
Massachusetts	House	7488	672	.090	137	137	7625	1.000	809	.106
	Senate	2458	137	.056	672	672	3130	1.000	809	.258
Michigan	House	1370	373	.272	147	76	1517	.517	449	.296
	Senate	610	147	.241	373	167	983	.448	314	.319
Minnesota	House	1540	261	.169	269	179	1809	.665	440	.243
	Senate	1476	269	.182	261	190	1737	.727	459	.264
Mississippi	House	1504	350	.213	277	272	1776	.018	597	.336
	Senate	1132	277	.240	350	320	1452	.094	622	.428

Table 4.1 (continued)

State	Chamber	# of Chamber Bills	# of Chamber Bills Passed	% Passed	# of Bills from Other Chamber	# of Bills from Other Chamber Passed	% Passed	Total Bills Received	Total Bills Passed	% Passed
Missouri	House	903	189	.209	103	74	.718	1006	263	.261
	Senate	458	103	.224	189	82	.434	647	185	.286
Montana	House	876	493	.563	339	268	.791	1215	761	.626
	Senate	486	339	.698	493	383	.777	979	722	.737
Nebraska	—	562	290	.516	—	—	—	562	290	.516
Nevada	House	710	434	.611	474	414	.873	1184	848	.716
	Senate	717	474	.661	434	368	.847	1151	842	.732
New Hampshire	House	955	553	.579	242	152	.628	1197	705	.589
	Senate	313	242	.773	553	443	.801	866	685	.791
New Jersey	House	847	234	.276	240	150	.625	1087	384	.353
	Senate	546	240	.440	234	196	.838	780	436	.559
New Mexico	House	723	381	.527	226	140	.619	949	521	.549
	Senate	488	226	.463	381	305	.801	869	531	.611
New York	House	9263	1385	.150	1516	687	.453	10779	2072	.192
	Senate	7210	1516	.210	1385	424	.306	8595	1940	.226
North Carolina	House	1384	847	.612	395	324	.820	1779	1171	.658
	Senate	772	395	.512	847	713	.842	1619	1108	.684
North Dakota	House	675	565	.837	378	282	.746	1053	847	.804
	Senate	441	378	.857	565	373	.660	1006	751	.747
Ohio	House	800	260	.325	93	43	.462	893	303	.339
	Senate	406	93	.229	260	101	.388	666	194	.291

State	Chamber									
Oklahoma	House	477	247	.818	219	148	.876	890	353	.808
	Senate	363	219	.603	247	209	.846	610	428	.702
Oregon	House	1368	618	.452	483	412	.853	1851	1030	.556
	Senate	1026	483	.471	618	533	.862	1644	1016	.618
Pennsylvania	House	2732	512	.187	391	287	.734	3123	799	.256
	Senate	1656	391	.236	512	356	.695	2168	747	.345
Rhode Island	House	1424	690	.485	696	377	.542	2120	1067	.503
	Senate	1190	696	.585	690	288	.417	1880	984	.523
South Carolina	House	818	432	.528	341	106	.311	1159	538	.464
	Senate	482	341	.707	432	166	.384	914	507	.555
South Dakota	House	383	281	.734	172	151	.878	555	432	.778
	Senate	248	172	.694	281	245	.872	529	417	.788
Tennessee	House	1426	488	.342	389	307	.789	1815	795	.438
	Senate	1456	389	.267	488	430	.881	1944	819	.421
Texas	House	2403	702	.292	551	391	.710	2954	1093	.370
	Senate	1293	551	.426	702	511	.728	1995	1062	.532
Utah	House	405	153	.378	219	161	.735	624	314	.503
	Senate	309	219	.709	153	152	.993	462	371	.803
Vermont	House	495	114	.230	63	36	.571	558	150	.269
	Senate	187	63	.337	114	82	.719	301	145	.482
Virginia	House	1837	549	.299	246	187	.760	2083	736	.353
	Senate	846	246	.291	549	482	.878	1395	728	.522
Washington	House	755	537	.711	506	214	.423	1261	751	.596
	Senate	1364	506	.371	537	142	.264	1901	648	.341
West Virginia	House	1100	192	.175	195	117	.600	1295	309	.239
	Senate	719	195	.271	192	111	.578	911	306	.336
Wisconsin	House	1161	326	.281	234	162	.692	1395	488	.350
	Senate	848	234	.276	326	250	.767	1174	484	.412
Wyoming	House	541	170	.314	142	71	.500	683	241	.353
	Senate	256	142	.555	170	116	.682	426	258	.606

Centralization

In general scholarly use, "centralization" normally refers to concentration of power or influence; it may be expressed in a number of other ways to suit specific language needs or personal preference. In bureaucracies, decentralization often means the delegation of decision-making authority to lower-level units. Corporations frequently centralize or decentralize through reorganization into a fewer or greater number of functional units. "Centralized decision making" usually means that decisions are made by few, whereas "decentralized decision making" usually means that decisions are made by many. In the legislative context, various types of decision making (e.g., gubernatorial, caucus, committee, subcommittee) may be indicative of greater or lesser centralization.

In the 1981 nationwide survey, state legislators were asked to indicate where they thought the most "significant decisions" were made. The question and results are illustrated in Table 4.2, which displays the total number of first, second, and third choices for each of eight categories of response. These responses can serve as the data base for developing a scale or index of centralization. Alternative procedures may be

Table 4.2   Legislator Perceptions of Significant Decision-Making
               Loci (Frequencies)

Q. In your legislature, where would you say the most significant decisions are made? Please use the numbers 1, 2, and 3 to order your top three choices, where "1" is your first choice.

Item	First Choice	Second Choice	Third Choice
Office of presiding officers or majority leaders	686	329	198
Regular committee meetings	496	459	338
Party caucus	340	291	307
In governor's office	171	270	215
On the floor	127	161	369
In policy committee	89	129	101
In subcommittees	44	95	106
Prelegislative session	20	43	41
Other or missing*	55	251	353

*Includes scattered responses and missing data. Most responses in this category in the second and third columns are "missing" (e.g., many legislators simply checked one item).

utilized to measure centralization. The one adopted here requires the use of parallelogram scaling of legislator responses for each chamber.

The scaling technique is explained in full in an earlier work (Jacoby and Francis, 1985). Briefly, the procedure (see Torgerson, 1958; Coombs, 1964) in this application utilizes the *modal* response set for each legislative chamber to reflect the *three most "significant" decision-making loci*. The modal response sets for all senate chambers are compared to all possible orderings of the response categories to achieve the most internally consistent scale alternative. The same procedure was applied to the house chambers. The final scale of items for both sets of chambers was identical, so that the ordinal arrangement turned out to be:

1. Governor's Office   MOST CENTRALIZED
2. Office of Presiding Officers or Majority Leaders
3. Party Caucus
4. Regular Committee Meetings
5. On the Floor
6. Subcommittees   LEAST CENTRALIZED

This result corresponds very well to an earlier three-point index of centralization constructed strictly on the basis of author judgment (Francis, 1967), where high centralization meant that significant decisions were said to occur in the governor's office or in policy committee, moderate centralization meant they were said to occur in party caucus, and low centralization meant that they were said to occur in regular committee meetings or on the floor. In this modern version, two new items are added:

1. Office of Presiding Officers or Majority Leaders
2. Subcommittees

One item, "in policy committee" does not scale well due to different meanings in different states and it is used only to modify the results in two state chambers, the Alaska and Oklahoma senates, where it appears the policy committees were leadership committees in 1981. The centralization scores for this ordinal scale are given in Table 4.3.

The modal response set of the three most significant decision-making centers introduces a more sophisticated way of viewing centralization. *Centralization is seen as a balance of different decision loci and not simply as the identification of a single important focus of activity.* As a confirmation of this perspective, a second measure of

Table 4.3   Decision-Making Centralization Scores for State
                Legislative Chambers

Scale Score	House Chambers	Senate Chambers
1		Alaska, Oklahoma
2	Alaska Delaware Indiana Iowa Maine New Jersey Pennsylvania South Dakota Illinois Massachusetts Michigan Minnesota North Carolina Ohio Rhode Island Tennessee Vermont Hawaii Maryland West Virginia California Oklahoma	Illinois Indiana Iowa Michigan Minnesota New Jersey Pennsylvania Rhode Island South Dakota Kentucky New Mexico North Carolina Oregon Texas Virginia Massachusetts
3	Arizona Colorado Connecticut Idaho New York North Dakota Utah Washington Wisconsin Kansas	Arizona Connecticut Idaho Kansas Maine Montana New York Ohio Tennessee Washington California Hawaii
4	Kentucky Montana New Mexico Wyoming Alabama Florida Missouri New Hampshire Oregon Texas Arkansas Louisiana Mississippi	Colorado Delaware Mississippi North Dakota Utah West Virginia Wisconsin Wyoming Alabama Florida Missouri Nevada New Hampshire Georgia Louisiana Vermont Maryland
	Nebraska	
5	Georgia Nevada South Carolina Virginia	Arkansas South Carolina

For exact pattern distinctions see Jacoby and Francis (1985, p 303). A scale score of 1 signifies
high centralization and a scale score of 5 indicates low centralization.

centralization-decentralization was employed on an experimental basis.
In this alternative scheme, decentralization was indexed simply by what
proportion of the time legislators gave "committee" or "subcommittee" responses as their first, second, or third choice (weighted accordingly). The alternative measure did not prove robust in further evaluation (i.e., did not perform well in regression experiments).

Control Variables

The degree of centralization is only one of several factors that may
affect the passage rate of legislative proposals. Included among the possible influences are:

1. Domination by the chair of the committee.
2. Committee scheduling and attendance problems.
3. Number of bills introduced.
4. Percent of members in the majority party.

The committee chairs play a key role in delaying legislation or moving it forward. As we saw earlier, key chairmen may form a management coalition with the elected leadership in order to promote and screen legislation. In the national survey, state legislators were asked to indicate whether the following statement characterized the way committees were managed in their chamber:

Most committees are dominated by the chairman.

Approximately 39 percent of the respondents indicated agreement with this item (See Appendix). We would expect that where the chairs dominate the committees the rank-and-file members would get their way less often and that legislation sponsored by them would have less success in moving to the next stage. In addition, the chairs may be in a governing coalition with the party leaders to restrict the legislative output. Chair domination can be measured for present purposes by calculating the percent of respondents from each chamber who endorsed the above statement.

The passage rate is likely to be affected also by the "procedural efficiency" of committee operations. Efficiency problems are indexed by another survey item in which legislators are asked whether:

For many members the schedule of meetings (committee-subcommittee) creates attendance problems.

As illustrated in Table 4.4, a substantial percent (43) of the legislators throughout the country indicated that this was a problem, and it was a problem recognized by both majority and minority party members. Procedural problems are indexed accordingly by the percent of members in each chamber who agree with the above statement.

While party discipline in most state legislatures is exercised only to a moderate degree, it would nevertheless seem to be an advantage for a majority member to have a sizeable plurality of party colleagues. The chamber plurality is no doubt reflected in committee and subcommittee memberships as well. Conventional wisdom on political party systems, however, would suggest that as one party becomes more dominant it tends to experience more factionalism. In a legislative setting it is apparent also that minority parties act with greater solidarity, and there is

Table 4.4 Identification of Committee System Problems

Problem	All Members	Majority Members	Minority Members
Most members receive too many committee assignments.	13	14	13
Many committees are too large to work effectively.	10	9	12
For many members the schedule of meetings (committee/ subcommittee) creates attendance problems.	43	42	47

Range of n = 1993–1999 for all members, 1301–1306 for majority members, 691–693 for minority party members.

some evidence to suggest that as a majority party increases in numbers beyond a safe margin it begins to have factional difficulties. The evidence in Figure 4.1 confirms this view to a point, but as we can see, parties with over 90 percent of the chamber membership seem to experience less factionalism. The drop in perceived factionalism in overwhelming majorities may be due to a number of factors, including the hopeless position of dissenters and the tendency to decentralize. In any

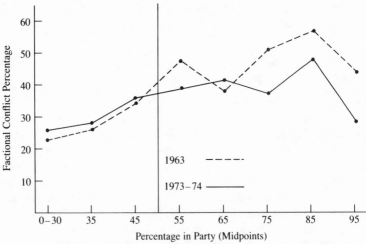

Fig. 4.1 Percentage of Legislator Responses Indicating Factional Conflict, by Representation of Their Parties in the Legislature

case, it is difficult to know whether such factionalism offsets the advantage of greater party pluralities in the various decision-making arenas.

The sheer volume of legislation can make it less likely that any single bill will pass. Most states are inundated by legislation, but some are inundated more than others. Legislators in most states do not have time to consider every piece of legislation. Thus, in order to understand the impact of centralization upon the passage rate, it is necessary to control for volume, which is expressed as the "number of bills introduced in the chamber of origin."

The Statistical Model

Letting the passage rate of bills in the house of origin serve as the dependent variable, the ordinary least squares model under investigation may be stated as:

$$\%PASS = a + b_1 (CENTR) + b_2(CHDOM) + b_3 (SCHED) \\ + b_4 (\#BILLS) + b_5 (\%MAJ) + e$$

where the centralization scale is employed as the first regressor and all impacts except possibly majority party percent ($\%MAJ$) are expected to depress the passage rate.

As we can observe in Table 4.5, all variables except perhaps "majority percent" exhibit a statistically discernable impact (normal criteria: $t > 2.0$ and $p < .05$) upon the chamber passage rate. Most important for the thesis developed here, centralization (as measured by the scaling procedure) appears to have a negative impact upon the passage rate. Decentralized decision making, we might speculate, is likely to be

Table 4.5 Variables Affecting the Chamber Passage Rate

Variable	b	t ratio	prob.	Standard-ized Beta
Centralization	−.03791	−2.31	.0234	−.201
Chair domination	−.26376	−2.25	.0271	−.215
Scheduling problems	−.15999	−2.37	.0197	−.215
Number of bills	−.00004	−3.23	.0017	−.288
Majority percent	.19009	1.49	.1406	.133

$\bar{R}^2 = .350$ Intercept = .41   N = 98 (Excludes Nebraska)

conducive to the formation of reciprocity norms and lead to higher passage rates. Predictably, chair domination, procedural inefficiency, and the volume of legislative proposals all have a negative impact upon the passage rate.

Congressional scholars may see problems with the above thesis. For example, many have noted the rise in importance of subcommittees over the last twenty years, a rise highlighted perhaps by the internal reorganizations in the House in the 1970s. At the same time, in both houses there have been declines in the number of bills passed and in the ratio of bills passed to bills introduced. Closer examination of data reported in the work of Ornstein, et al. (1984), however, reveals a somewhat different picture.

In both houses of Congress, the passage rate began to decline as early as 1950 and reached its low point in the early 1970s, just before the impact of the new emphasis upon subcommittee autonomy. During the same extended period, the content of legislation became much more detailed and complex. As recently as the Eighty-Seventh Congress (1961–62) approximately two thousand pages of bills were enacted, with an average of 2.3 pages per statute, but by the Ninety-Seventh Congress (1981–82) over forty-three hundred pages of bills were enacted with an average of 9.2 pages per statute. The increase has been most dramatic since 1973, about the time when members began asserting their rights in committees and subcommittees.

The passage rate is only one alternative for detecting the impact of reciprocal arrangements. Small subcommittees may have the capacity to merge varied interests in the group into fewer pieces of legislation. Alternatively, there may be a "crowding-out" effect. Since bills are now more detailed, they take longer to negotiate and "mark up." Since there is a finite amount of time available, more bills will fail to receive a subcommittee hearing. In any case, a test of the validity of these alternative explanations requires an examination of Congressional subcommittees and their success.

Decentralization appears to produce greater output. In most states such output is detectable in the passage rate, while in Congress the volume of processed legislation is perhaps better indexed by the number of pages. The effects of decentralization are modified, of course, by other factors such as inefficiency.

It is reasonable to question at this point in the analysis the overall significance of a measure such as the passage rate. After all, legislators have official activities other than getting their bills passed. In Congress, constituency service and legislative oversight of administrative agencies are normally considered to be major categories of legislator responsibility. The results of this study are consistent with the conclusions of Rosenthal and Forth (1978) and Elling (1979)—oversight is not very important when compared to "legislating" in the states. When surveyed legislators were asked to divide up their committee and subcommittee work into hours spent on each of several activities, they allocated only thirty minutes a day to "reviewing the conduct of administrative agencies." In contrast they allocated nearly four hours a day to legislating, which includes (See Table 7.1 for detail):

a. Obtaining information about proposals in order to understand their content.

b. Finding out how other members feel about the issues.

c. Hammering out workable compromises with members of committees.

Only in Connecticut, Hawaii, Idaho, Maryland, and New Mexico, and in the Michigan senate do respondents indicate they spend an hour a day reviewing administrative agencies (although see Hamm and Robertson, 1981). These are also states (except Michigan) in which legislators spend much more time on committee work as a whole.

In sum, state legislators spend the lion's share of their time working with legislation. The passage rate focuses directly on this activity by reflecting bill sponsorship success. Bill sponsorship success is depressed by a number of structural factors, including the degree to which decision making is centralized, the degree to which the chairs dominate the committees, and the scheduling inefficiency of the organization. That is, even when we control statistically for the quantity of legislation introduced, each of these structural factors appears to have a net negative impact upon success rates.

While individual sponsorship of bills in most states is a serious business, it is conceivable that the nature of legislative business in the states is evolving away from the traditional way of doing things. Sponsorship action may become secondary to committee negotiations on important legislation, or to the development of "committee" bills of omnibus proportions. In any case, the question deserves further analysis. A severe test can be applied by asking whether the "passage rate" is a major factor in the extent to which legislators are satisfied overall with legislative session outcomes. Legislators come away from legislative sessions with varying degrees of satisfaction, depending in part on how the legislative experience measures up in comparison with other opportunities. These broader questions of satisfaction and career evaluation are taken up in the next section, part two of this book.

Part Two

Lifestyle and Career-Pattern Influences

5

Costs and Benefits of Legislative Service

The previous chapter identified a number of factors that lead to a higher success rate on legislative proposals, including procedural efficiency, decentralization, and a lack of committee chair domination. One severe limitation of such an approach, however, is that it provides only a microscopic view of what makes a difference in the conduct of legislative business. From the whole life perspective of the legislator, the benefits of greater success on legislation can be offset by the personal costs of achieving such success. This chapter and the next take into account the overall perspective of the legislator, whose responsibilities go well beyond the official duties of the job.

More specifically, in this chapter the extent to which legislators are satisfied with legislative outcomes is shown to be a function of:

1. Success rates on legislation.
2. Number of workdays.

These are seen as proxies for the benefits and costs of legislative service. The number of workdays is important because legislators suffer opportunity costs in the nonpublic sector.

When compared to the diversity of legislative practices throughout the world, the American state legislatures in many respects appear to be

The author has published parts of this chapter in "Costs and Benefits of Legislative Service in the American States." *American Journal of Political Science* (1985) 29:626–642. Published by University of Texas Press.

the institutional cousins of Congress. In at least one important respect, however, they do differ. Most state legislatures are still part-time legislatures. In two-thirds of the states there are constitutional limits to the length of the session and, in 1981, for example, only eleven states held more than one hundred session workdays, with Massachusetts topping the list at 177. It is true that the states do hold special sessions or assign interim committees to responsibilities that extend the duties of members beyond the regular session, and in the last twenty years we have also witnessed longer and more frequent sessions. Nevertheless, even now, most state legislators cannot rely on legislative compensation alone and have another occupation.

Recent pressures toward professionalization and modernization have created a situation where legislators must consider carefully the costs and benefits of their endeavors. Essentially legislators are concerned about the costs, or how much work they must put into the system to obtain the benefits derived from the legislation they sponsor. The purpose of this chapter is to demonstrate the significance of this cost-benefit perspective and to evaluate legislative practices that are related to it.

To pursue the above purpose, this analysis relies upon three major sources of information, each of which applies to *regular* sessions only:

1. The number of days spent in legislative session (workdays), obtained by surveying legislative service personnel for a monthly breakdown of workdays (1981).

2. The number of bills introduced and passed by each chamber, obtained from official documents and qualified state librarians and legislative service personnel (1981).

3. Questionnaire returns from over two thousand state legislators representing all ninety-nine chambers (1981).

4. Salary, compensation, and length of session information for two periods in time (early 1960s and early 1980s).

These sources combine individual survey data with information taken from official and semiofficial records.

Legislative Workdays

The "costs" of legislative decision making refer to both the time and the energy members devote to their official duties, but measurement limitations usually require that we examine only *time costs*. With respect to time costs, state legislators may be quite different from their Congressional counterparts. Members who enter Congress expect to be full-time lawmakers, but most state legislators are so-called "citizen" legislators. They have a private occupation, an income-producing activity that may be reduced by service in the state capital. For those who are not full-time "professional" legislators, the opportunity costs of serving in the state legislature are often substantial. The state income paid to state legislators is typically quite modest and, over and above expenses, is normally fixed.

Because of opportunity costs, state legislators will be quite concerned with the number of workdays required of them during the legislative session. The actual number of regular session workdays estimated for each chamber is displayed in Table 5.1. As we can see, the number varies substantially in 1981—30 to 40 workdays in Florida, Georgia, New Jersey, Virginia, and Wyoming to 120 or more in Alaska, California, Massachusetts, North Carolina, Ohio, Oregon, and South Carolina. The mean number of workdays is 75, with a standard deviation of 32. These workdays, of course, fall within a much longer calendar period, ranging over the entire year in a few states.

The measure employed in this study may be referred to as the number of regular session workdays. This information was obtained by surveying legislative service personnel. They were provided with a chart so that they could indicate in detail the actual days per week their legislatures met. The great variety of legislative practices serves as a caution against using only the official starting and ending dates of the sessions. Vacation breaks, one-day, two-day, three-day, four-day, and full work weeks are all very common. The number of days a legislator is required to spend in the state capitol would seem to be the best indicator of stress that might arise due to occupational and other responsibilities in the home district.

The tension between public and private occupational duties is reported, for example, by Jewell (1982) in reflecting upon his personal interviews with 221 legislators in nine states:

It was obvious from my interviews that it has become increasingly difficult for members to serve half-time. On the one hand, the pressures of the legislative job push the members to enlarge their commitment of time beyond 50-percent. On the other hand, members learn that it is very difficult to be a 50-percent teacher, or businessman, or lawyer. It is even more difficult to maintain an outside career when you can devote only 30 to 40 percent of your time to it. (p. 186)

Table 5.1   Number of Workdays, 1981: State Legislative Chambers

State	House	Senate	State	House	Senate
Alabama	45	45	Montana	90	90
*Alaska	120	120	Nebraska	90	
Arizona	64	64	Nevada	103	103
Arkansas	47	42	New Hampshire	48	48
*California	128	128	*New Jersey	32	32
*Colorado	107	107	New Mexico	46	46
Connecticut	95	95	*New York	69	69
Delaware	52	52	*North Carolina	127	127
Florida	32	26	North Dakota	60	60
Georgia	40	40	*Ohio	125	116
Hawaii	63	63	Oklahoma	86	86
*Idaho	55	55	*Oregon	143	143
*Illinois	83	82	*Pennsylvania	59	55
Indiana	84	84	Rhode Island	67	67
Iowa	85	86	*South Carolina	123	123
*Kansas	82	82	South Dakota	42	42
Kentucky	60	60	Tennessee	64	64
Louisiana	54	48	Texas	83	83
*Maine	103	103	Utah	45	45
Maryland	65	65	Vermont	72	72
*Massachusetts	177	176	Virginia	30	30
*Michigan	108	105	Washington	72	72
Minnesota	57	57	West Virginia	43	43
Mississippi	70	70	*Wisconsin	61	64
Missouri	97	97	Wyoming	40	40

*No Session Limit Set Either by Constitution or Pay Structure

Only twenty years ago most state legislatures met every other year, and usually for less time in the year that they did meet. By 1980, a mere handful of states still employed the biennial session. The tension between public and private responsibilities built up during this period. Many states now pay legislators more than they once did, but the differences are often unthinkingly exaggerated by not taking into account the purchasing power of the dollar and the additional number of days most legislators now devote to official business. New Hampshire still pays only $100 per year and Alabama $10 per day. As of 1981, no state paid as much as $30,000 per year in regular salary. A recent *Congressional*

Quarterly study, for example, noted that modest pay and longer sessions seem to be attracting a different type of legislator (CQ *Weekly Report*, 1983, pp. 1768–769), those from modest-paying occupations and those young enough (or old enough) to find the salary level tolerable.

Bill Passage Rates

The "benefits" in legislative decision making are derived no doubt in a number of ways, but it is important to understand that in contrast to Congress a great proportion of legislative time in the states is spent in law production (Rosenthal and Forth, 1978). While casework and oversight are important, they are nevertheless not as central as law production to the official duties of the state legislator. Because law production is so central, the agendas of the various participants become especially crucial. The agendas of the governor and chamber party leaders are most often at the front end of legislative business, but realistically, as previously shown, it would be better to assume that each member has an agenda or at least identifies with an agenda. The agendas of all legislators may be seen as changing and overlapping and in competition for scarce time and attention.

The passage rates necessarily have the weakness of indexing only the proportion of wins, not the value of such wins. Legislators may win on many minor proposals, but lose on a few major proposals. To acquire insight into this problem, it is possible to consult directly the responses of legislators to the following question:

> How *satisfied* were you with those *bills that were passed or recommended favorably* by the following units of your legislature?

The "unit" in question here is "my chamber as a whole," on which legislators registered a response on a five-point scale ranging from "very high" satisfaction to "very low" satisfaction (See Appendix). As a backup, legislators were also asked:

> How *satisfied* were you with the decisions *not to consider, recommend unfavorably, or defeat* bills by the following units?

The same response categories were provided. Examination of these satisfaction levels should aid in understanding the impact of the number of session workdays and the bill passage rate.

The number of legislative measures introduced or passed has served as a form of evidence in several earlier studies of legislative behavior, both at the individual level (Matthews, 1959; Francis, 1962) and at the aggregate level (Hedlund and Hamm, 1978; Hedlund and Freeman, 1981). Hedlund and Freeman, for example, discussed legislative "efficiency" in terms of "bills passed per session day" or "bills introduced per session day." The present analysis differs from theirs in two respects. First, session days are treated here as a separate variable (as a proxy for costs). Second, the number of bills passed are taken as a proportion of the number introduced to offer the passage rate as a proxy for benefits. More formally, Hedlund and Freeman proposed that legislative efficiency (L) is a function of a number of variables, such that $L = f(p/s, i/s, \ldots)$. Here it is suggested that legislative satisfaction level (T) is a function of a number of variables, such that $T = f(1/s, p/i, \ldots)$, where s is the number of session days, p the number of bills passed, and i the number of bills introduced.

Majority Party Satisfaction with Outcomes: A Test

Since in all states but Nebraska the legislature is organized and controlled by the majority party, member satisfaction with chamber outcomes will be influenced by party status. For example, on a five-point scale of satisfaction with bills passed by the chamber, there was a 0.54 scale difference between the mean score for minority members (n = 650) and the mean score for majority members (n = 1268). Minority party members naturally are less satisfied with legislative outcomes. In the analysis to follow, only majority party responses will be evaluated. While minority party responses ultimately will need to be assessed, several factors weigh in favor of examining majority party members only at this point. First, the response rate and/or the number of minority party members in many chambers yields too few observations for a chamber-by-chamber aggregation. Second, inclusion of minority party responses can confound the analysis because of the adversarial partisan role such members may play. Third, it is the majority party and its leadership that run the chamber and manage its business, and thus it seems more important to understand first their reactions to the environment.

The purpose of this section is to evaluate the relationship between majority party satisfaction with outcomes and the actual days of legislative work and the bill passage rate of each chamber. Each chamber is assigned a mean satisfaction rating based upon majority party member responses to the previously illustrated survey questions. This will allow a direct comparison with other chamber-level data. The aggregated ratings are given in Table 5.2. Since it was not possible to measure workdays and the passage rate at the individual level, the satisfaction responses are aggregated. The purpose here is not to analyze individual satisfaction, but to confirm that the days of work and the bill passage rate are important characteristics of the legislative chamber. Accordingly, ordinary least squares (OLS) provides appropriate estimates in the subsequent analysis.

Variation in sample size from chamber to chamber, as detailed in Table 5.2, caused concern because of the possible impact upon residuals (i.e., variance inversely related to sample size), but application of the Goldfeld and Quandt (1965) test for heteroskedasticity indicated that weighted least squares (WLS) was not necessary and that the OLS estimates would be appropriate.

By choice this analysis controls for one of the more important variables determining legislator satisfaction with outcomes—that of majority-minority party status. In other words, beyond the impact of party status, what variables have an impact upon legislator satisfaction ratings of outcomes? In the initial preparatory analysis it was found that majority party satisfaction with decisions to pass or defeat bills correlated negatively with the number of workdays ($r = -0.43$ and -0.40) and positively with the percentage of bills passed by the chamber ($r = 0.32$ and 0.35). A check of the complete intercorrelation matrix compiled for this new data set revealed that these were the highest zero order correlations with "majority party satisfaction" in a pool of seventy-eight original and derived variables. Estimated in equation terms, we may let

MAJSATP = Majority party member mean satisfaction rating for bills passed.

MAJSATD = Majority party member mean satisfaction rating for decisions to defeat bills.

WKDAYS = Number of 1981 regular session workdays (1980 for Kentucky).

%PASS = Proportion of bills passing the chamber (includes bills from both houses here).

where

Table 5.2   Majority Member Satisfaction Ratings of Outcomes (Mean Scores)*

	House: Decisions to			Senate: Decisions to		
State	*Pass*	*Not Pass*	*Pop.*	*Pass*	*Not Pass*	*Pop*
Alabama	2.9(15)	3.1(13)	100	2.5(11)	2.6(9)	35
Alaska	3.4(7)	3.0(7)	22	3.0(4)	3.3(4)	11
Arizona	2.5(22)	2.5(20)	43	2.6(9)	2.7(9)	16
Arkansas	2.7(22)	2.7(21)	93	2.3(8)	2.7(7)	34
California	2.7(9)	2.4(9)	48	2.5(4)	2.5(4)	23
Colorado	2.8(22)	2.8(19)	39	2.6(5)	2.6(5)	22
Connecticut	2.7(12)	2.8(10)	83	2.3(7)	2.6(7)	22
Delaware	2.6(14)	2.8(10)	25	2.8(4)	2.5(2)	12
Florida	1.9(17)	1.8(14)	81	2.4(7)	2.3(7)	27
Georgia	2.2(17)	2.3(16)	156	2.4(10)	2.7(9)	51
Hawaii	2.8(16)	2.9(15)	39	2.4(9)	2.8(8)	17
Idaho	2.4(29)	2.6(28)	56	2.2(13)	2.4(13)	23
Illinois	2.7(16)	2.7(16)	91	2.0(3)	2.0(3)	30
Indiana	2.5(19)	2.6(19)	63	2.1(14)	2.1(14)	35
Iowa	2.8(18)	2.9(16)	58	2.3(12)	2.3(12)	28
Kansas	2.7(22)	2.5(22)	72	2.5(12)	2.5(11)	24
Kentucky	2.6(19)	2.5(15)	75	2.3(10)	2.5(11)	29
Louisiana	2.4(14)	2.7(12)	95	2.0(9)	1.8(8)	39
Maine	2.5(11)	2.5(11)	84	2.3(7)	2.6(7)	17
Maryland	2.6(28)	2.6(27)	125	2.4(14)	2.2(13)	40
Massachusetts	3.2(12)	3.0(12)	128	3.3(3)	3.3(3)	32
Michigan	2.4(12)	2.8(11)	64	3.3(4)	2.7(3)	24
Minnesota	2.3(9)	3.0(9)	70	2.4(10)	2.6(10)	45
Mississippi	2.8(20)	3.0(19)	115	2.4(10)	2.3(9)	48
Missouri	3.0(19)	3.0(18)	111	3.3(4)	2.7(3)	23
Montana	2.5(24)	2.4(23)	57	2.3(7)	2.4(7)	29
Nebraska				2.7(29)	3.1(20)	49
Nevada	2.6(13)	2.5(12)	26	2.4(7)	2.9(7)	15
New Hampshire	2.7(16)	2.5(14)	238	3.2(6)	2.7(6)	13
New Jersey	2.8(13)	2.6(11)	44	2.1(7)	2.1(7)	25
New Mexico	2.8(19)	2.9(17)	41	2.8(6)	2.8(5)	22
New York	2.4(13)	2.6(14)	86	2.7(3)	2.7(3)	35
North Carolina	2.4(21)	2.5(19)	95	2.5(11)	2.6(11)	40
North Dakota	2.1(31)	2.3(27)	73	2.2(12)	2.3(11)	40

Table 5.2   (*continued*)

State	House: Decisions to			Senate: Decisions to		
	Pass	*Not Pass*	*Pop.*	*Pass*	*Not Pass*	*Pop.*
Ohio	2.6(17)	2.6(12)	54	2.7(6)	2.5(6)	18
Oklahoma	2.7(12)	2.6(12)	73	2.5(6)	2.7(6)	37
Oregon	3.0(13)	3.2(13)	33	2.4(8)	2.7(7)	22
Pennsylvania	2.4(8)	2.6(8)	103	2.6(5)	3.0(4)	25
Rhode Island	2.4(18)	2.6(17)	82	2.5(6)	2.8(5)	43
South Carolina	2.8(21)	2.8(19)	107	2.5(10)	2.8(10)	41
South Dakota	2.3(26)	2.4(24)	49	2.4(14)	2.0(14)	25
Tennessee	2.3(8)	2.5(8)	57	2.3(7)	2.5(6)	20
Texas	2.6(19)	3.0(18)	114	2.8(10)	2.8(9)	23
Utah	2.6(25)	2.6(25)	58	2.3(12)	2.3(11)	22
Vermont	2.6(10)	3.0(8)	86	2.2(5)	2.3(3)	16
Virginia	2.5(20)	2.5(19)	74	2.0(7)	2.1(7)	31
Washington	2.4(19)	2.4(18)	56	2.2(10)	2.4(7)	25
West Virginia	2.4(18)	2.5(17)	78	2.4(9)	2.6(9)	27
Wisconsin	2.8(18)	2.8(20)	59	2.6(5)	2.6(5)	19
Wyoming	2.4(26)	2.4(25)	39	2.5(10)	2.6(10)	19

*In each case (n) = the number of respondents and the population is the number of majority party members in the chamber.

$$MAJSATP = 2.478 - .0036(WKDAYS) + .4203(\%PASS) \quad 5.1$$

$\bar{R}^2 = .232$	$t = -4.33$	$t = 2.81$
$N = 99$	$p < .001$	$p < .006$
	$B = -.389$	$B = .252$

$$MAJSATD = 2.603 - .0032(WKDAYS) + .4769(\%PASS) \quad 5.2$$

$\bar{R}^2 = .229$	$t = -3.90$	$t = 3.28$
$N = 99$	$p < .001$	$p < .001$
	$B = -.351$	$B < .295$

Thus, the fewer the workdays, the lower the time costs of participating in the legislature. The greater the passage rate, the greater the benefits achieved while participating.

Examination of the above relationship for each chamber reveals only one severe outlier, that of the New Hampshire Senate. Respondents

of the Republican majority in this 23-member chamber (in 1981) con-
veyed dissatisfaction in spite of few workdays (48) and a high passage
rate (.791). Whether the exception was caused by measurement or sam-
pling error (6 of 13 responded), or stochastic disturbances cannot be determined, but as is normal the regression estimates are probably more
accurate if the single case is set aside and the equations are restated
as follows:

$$\text{MAJSATP} = 2.496 - .0038(\text{WKDAYS})$$
$$+ .5027(\%\text{PASS})$$ 5.3

$$\bar{R}^2 = .291 \qquad t = -4.83 \qquad t = 3.53$$
$$N = 98 \qquad p < .001 \qquad p < .001$$
$$B = -.417 \qquad B = .305$$

$$\text{MAJSATD} = 2.613 - .0032(\text{WKDAYS})$$
$$+ .5071(\%\text{PASS})$$ 5.4

$$\bar{R}^2 = .241 \qquad t = -3.99 \qquad t = 3.45$$
$$N = 98 \qquad p < .001 \qquad p < .001$$
$$B = -.357 \qquad B = .309$$

The fact that the equation estimates for passed legislation and defeated
legislation are so similar gives confirmation to the overall interpretation
that the passage rate and the number of workdays are important in legislator assessments of chamber success. It seems reasonable to speculate,
however, that other factors are also at work. For example, constitutional
or statutory limits, or even specific legislative rules, may influence the
above stated relationships. As of 1981, there were seventeen states without a constitutional or pay limit on the length of the legislative session
(See Table 5.1). Of the remaining states, six had pay limits only, and
twenty-seven had constitutional limits on either the number of calendar
days, the number of legislative days, or both (Council of State Governments, 1980, pp. 108–109).

The state chambers without a constitutional limit in 1981 spent an
average of one hundred workdays in session, whereas those with limits
held to an average of sixty-three regular session workdays. This relationship is expressed in a correlation of 0.55 between the number of
workdays and the limit-versus-no-limit dichotomy. When controlling
for the number of workdays, however, formal limits on the length of the
session appear to have no direct impact upon chamber majority party
satisfaction ratings. For example, the appropriate model of satisfaction
with those that passed is:

where it may be seen that it is the number of workdays that affects the ratings (N = 98).

As a final consideration here we can determine whether a multiplicative term should be added to the above regression models. That is, we may wish to know whether the slope of the regression of satisfaction ratings on the passage rate increases or decreases with the number of workdays. If such an "interactive" effect is apparent, then the appropriate multiplicative term should be added to the model. Letting the product of the two regressors, WKDAYS and %PASS, be represented by the term D×P, the two resulting equations are:

$$\text{MAJSATP} = 2.186 - .0077(\text{WKDAYS}) \\ - .1587(\%\text{PASS}) + .0087(\text{D}\times\text{P})$$

5.5

$\bar{R}^2 = .321$	$t = -4.05$	$t = -.491$	$t = 2.27$
$N = 98$	$p < .001$	$p < .624$	$p < .026$

$$\text{MAJSATD} = 2.553 - .004(\text{WKDAYS}) \\ + .3851(\%\text{PASS}) + .0016(\text{D}\times\text{P})$$

5.6

$\bar{R}^2 = .234$	$t = -1.96$	$t = 1.13$	$t = .40$
$N = 98$	$p < .053$	$p < .263$	$p < .694$

The Goldfeld and Quandt test indicated that heteroskedasticity was not apparent in these equations.

It may be observed that for decisions to defeat legislation, the multiplicative term is not significant ($t = .40$), and the adjusted multiple coefficient of determination remains virtually the same as it was before adding the new term. The ratings of satisfaction with passed legislation, however, do reveal both a significant multiplicative term and an improved $\bar{R}^2$. The coefficients for the original independent terms are *conditional* rather than *general* coefficients in these equations and must be interpreted as such (See Friedrich, 1982). Equation 5.5 suggests that the passage rate better explains majority member satisfaction in those states that have a greater number of workdays. The most apparent reason for this phenomenon is that in the chambers of a few states with short sessions, the bill success rate may be high enough to signify a less careful approach to bill consideration. As a consequence, individuals in those chambers may feel that the success of their own agenda is more than offset by the success of ill-advised legislation. If this interpretation is correct, the outlier senate of New Hampshire would serve as the extreme case, where twenty-three members passed 685 bills (79%) in forty-eight workdays. Less obvious but similar patterns were noted for one or both chambers in New Mexico, Arkansas, Delaware, and Alabama.

In summary, the previous analysis has demonstrated that the number of workdays and the passage rate are important factors in explaining majority party satisfaction with legislative outcomes. In the state legislative context of mostly part-time service, the workdays create ample opportunity costs, and legislators will weigh their experience in light of these costs. The importance of the passage rate as an indicator of legislator satisfaction may reflect also the specific nature of *state* legislative decision making, where law production is dominant. We would expect that legislators obtain gratification also by getting their "two cents worth" in omnibus bills, but the overall volume of processed legislation would imply that the so-called minor bills, by their very numbers, occupy a major share of the legislators' time and energy.

Perhaps the most appropriate way to think of the "number of workdays" and the "passage rate" is that they are proxies for the *costs* and *benefits* of legislative service. The principal cost to most state legislators is the number of days they need to spend in the state capital. The principal benefit is their success rate on legislative proposals (and the kinds of rewards such success brings). A reasonable assumption about human behavior is that members of groups want the most benefits at the least cost, and the state legislature is no exception.

The Dilemma

The state legislature is distinguished often from Congress because of its part-time status. The distinction is of long-standing recognition, and most reformers have recommended an increase in the length of legislative sessions. The study of the Citizens Conference on State Legislatures, *The Sometime Governments*, for example, recommends the removal of constitutional restrictions on session time and interim work (1971, p. 156). Slowly but surely the transition from part-time to full-time legislatures is occurring. Whether this evolution will continue to completion is difficult to determine. It is evident now that the transition

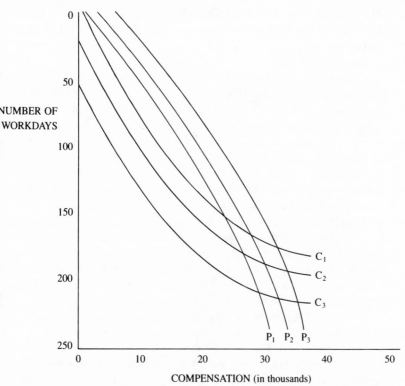

Fig. 5.1   Indifference (or Preference) Curves of "Citizen" and
              "Professional" Legislators

has brought with it a serious source of tension between public and private employment. It has become very difficult to serve two masters, especially when each demands of the legislator better than 50 percent of his or her time. The impact of this phenomenon is illustrated dramatically by the extent to which the days of work of legislators seem to influence negatively their evaluations of chamber performance.

As suggested earlier, many legislators have opportunity costs that make lengthy service at the state capital undesirable. We might presume, of course, that higher salaries or compensation could offset these costs. Because many legislators are not willing to give up their private occupations or careers, it may be difficult to retain them at any cost. Continuance in public office is not assured. The trade-offs are illustrated in Figure 5.1 through indifference curves C_1, C_2, and C_3. Following conventional economic analysis, any two points on a single indifference curve are of equal value to the individual in question. Thus if a legislator's indifference curve is C_1, C_2, or C_3, he would need to receive a higher *rate* of pay as the number of workdays increases in order to offset the opportunity costs.

In contrast, however, a substantial number of legislators may not have income producing activities in the private sector. It is in their interest to increase *total* compensation. These "professional" legislators see the legislative position as a full-time job, and in the extreme they may be willing to accept a lower rate of pay in exchange for greater total compensation. The indifference curves for this type of legislator are illustrated in Figure 5.1 (P_1, P_2, P_3). In reality, of course, we would expect legislators to be arrayed in a continuum, from those with highly concave indifference curves to those with convex indifference curves, depending upon the extent of their opportunities in the private sector.

To gain perspective, a twenty-two year period, from 1962 to 1984, should serve as an adequate span of time to note changes in compensation and legislative session obligations. During this period legislative compensation (salaries plus per diem) increased from a mean of $5,552 to a mean of $10,296 in deflated dollars (by ⅓, using cost of living index), or by 85.4 percent. But during approximately this same period, the number of days in legislative session (actual workdays not available) increased from a mean of 174 to a mean of 277, or an increase of 59.3 percent. In aggregate terms, then, the real increase in pay was only about 26 percent. State-by-state detail reveals that compensation per day-in-session appears to have decreased in twenty-one states. In many states, therefore, compensation has not kept up with increases in legislative obligation. In addition, in many states the increases in the rate of pay would seem inadequate to satisfy legislators with substantial opportunity costs.

These results point to the need to examine more carefully the recruitment and retirement patterns of legislators under emerging conditions as the state legislatures become more "professional" in orientation. To shed some light on the subject, the following chapter is a study of retirement patterns in our two case study states, Indiana and Missouri. A second concern is whether the legislative experience itself is rewarding enough to offset what may be the benefits of other endeavors.

6

Self-Interest and Legislative Turnover

Decisions of legislators to run for reelection or retire from office have attracted scholarly attention for a variety of reasons. In the study of Congress, for example, the goal of winning reelection has become the driving assumption in explaining much of Congressional behavior, including the emphasis on casework, positioning on committees and subcommittees, issue selection, expense allowances, and in general the success of members against most challengers (Fenno, 1973; Mayhew, 1974; Kingdon, 1977, Fiorina, 1977). For Congress, the goal of winning reelection, while not universally pursued by members (e.g., see Cooper and West, 1981; Hibbing, 1982), seems to be nevertheless a dominant motivation. Most observers of Congress worry about the lack of turnover and the "insulation" of members.

Almost by tradition, the concern of state legislative observers has been the very opposite. High turnover rather than low turnover is the cause for concern. The historical basis for this concern is demonstrated in Ray's (1974) three-state study of Connecticut, Michigan, and Wisconsin. He demonstrates that at the turn of the century the turnover rates in these three states were between 60 and 80 percent. By the 1930s the turnover rate in ten state houses was estimated at slightly less than 40

Much of this chapter appeared in an article that was written while the book was in progress. See Wayne L. Francis and John R. Baker, "Why Do U.S. State Legislators Vacate Their Seats?" *Legislative Studies Quarterly* 11 (1986): 119–126.

percent (Hyneman, 1938), but by the 1960s estimates were still in excess of 35 percent (Rosenthal, 1974b). In most recent years (1978–82), the rates have declined further, and as pointed out by Wiggins and Bernick (1977), the problem of turnover is no longer so apparent. Recent data indicate that the turnover rate ranges from approximately 25 to 32 percent (Council of State Governments, 1980–1984). Incentives for reelection do vary considerably from state to state, and they may be changing as states make changes in compensation and session requirements.

There are two basic reasons why scholars become concerned with high turnover. First, the legislature may lack the experienced members necessary to manage its business efficiently. Expertise is needed in committee negotiations, and in general it helps to have "a memory" of the procedures of government and of past decisions. Second, high turnover may reflect the inability to recruit or retain quality members, which suggests further that there may be a problem in the incentive structure. That is, if members exit the legislature because they were defeated in the primary or general election, so be it. That is the way the game is played. But if they leave for other reasons, it will pay to take a closer look at the problem.

One principal reason for a member to leave office voluntarily is to challenge another candidate for a more desirable position. In 1957, a four-state interview study of California, Ohio, New Jersey, and Tennessee revealed that more than one-third of nearly five hundred legislators had definite aspirations to higher office and another one-fourth thought that running for higher office was at least a possibility (Eulau, et al., in Marvick, 1961, p. 255). Following up on the careers of these members through 1971, Hain (1974) has shown that "progressive ambitions" are highly related to age. More important for our purposes here is Hain's verification that a high percentage of state legislators in fact do seek "higher" office. In the original sample, 59 percent expressed progressive ambitions. Hain found that 44 percent actually did seek another office.

Decisions to leave the legislature may be due to a number of factors. Blair and Henry (1981), for example, examined fifty-six voluntary retirees who did not run immediately for another office. They found that personal factors (especially family related) were the most frequently cited (82%), but that professional (48%) and political (23%) factors were apparent also. Even those who did run immediately for another office may have had other reasons for their exit. Thus, the decision to leave can be seen as a complex weighing of the costs and benefits of the available alternatives. It is the purpose of this chapter to investigate this decision process.

The 1981–82 memberships of the Indiana and Missouri legislatures provide the data for this examination. Serving in those years were 50 members of the Indiana senate and 99 members of the house. Missouri had 34 senate and 163 house members. Both chambers of Indiana were controlled by Republicans, whereas the Democrats had their typical large majorities in the Missouri legislature. In 1981 the average number of "workdays" in all state legislatures was 75. Indiana had 84 workdays and Missouri had 97. Annual legislative salaries plus expenses were estimated at $11,000 for Indiana and $18,400 for Missouri. For all states the mean salary plus expense level is estimated at $13,500 for 1981. Special sessions allow a per diem but no additional salary. In 1981 Indiana spent three days in special session, whereas Missouri spent about ten days. Total compensation per day of work is estimated at $127 for Indiana and $129 for Missouri.

Slightly more than 25 percent of the 1981–82 membership did not return for the 1983–84 term. Excluding those senators who were not up for reelection, 29 percent were either defeated or left office. By chamber these turnover figures are:

Indiana House	26%
Senate	36% (9 of 25)
Missouri House	29%
Senate	41% (7 of 17)

In these two states a total of 89 members did not return for the 1983 session. Of the 89, 63 left for reasons other than election defeat. In other words, about 71 percent of the turnover is due to reasons other than election defeat. This compares to 63 percent for the Blair and Henry data for Arkansas for 1970–78, 63–70 percent for the multistate data of Calvert (1979) for 1966–76, and 68.5 percent for the early Hyneman data.

The sixty-three members of the Indiana and Missouri legislatures who voluntarily retired in 1982 were sent questionnaires in an attempt to evaluate their decisions. Of these members, forty-three (68%) responded satisfactorily.[1] In the central question, legislators were asked to

---

1. In Indiana 36% (9 of 25) of the voluntary retirees were from the minority party. This compares to 34% for the entire legislative membership. In Missouri 42% (16 of 38) were from the minority party, compared to 32% for the full membership. Among the returns from retired members, minority party members constituted 21% of the total for Indiana and 41% for Missouri. Although we might suspect that minority party members would

indicate which of the following reasons were appropriate in explaining their decision not to seek reelection:

a. Decided to run for another office.

b. Health or retirement.

c. Dissatisfaction with legislative experience (or the legislature).

d. Needed to spend more time in my private occupation or business.

e. Was offered a more attractive career position.

f. Family needs.

g. Adverse political circumstances in my district.

h. Other _____.

Respondents could give more than one reason, and more than half did. Where possible, responses in "h" were recoded in "a" through "g."

In order to better comprehend the diverse responses to the above question, the results have been organized under five main categories:

1. Opportunity Costs.

2. Legislative Dissatisfaction.

3. Career Ambitions.

4. Health or Normal Retirement Age.

5. Electoral Expectations.

Opportunity costs are those benefits that legislators forego because they must serve in the legislature. Most legislators in the states under study (and probably in most other states as well) have private occupations or businesses that both produce income and require at least part of their time and energy. Workdays in the state capitol take legislators away from these income producing activities. Workdays in the state capitol also take many legislators away from their families and those benefits that come in the form of leisure and personal satisfaction in the home or family environment.

Of the forty-three respondents in this study, seventeen were classified as indicating that opportunity costs were important in their decisions to leave. The frequencies can be illustrated as follows:

---

have greater reason to voluntarily retire, the above evidence gives only weak (if any) support to this notion. In examining reasons for retirement, as discussed later, majority-minority status was not found to illustrate major differences with sufficient statistical certainty, although with a larger N a number of distinctions may emerge.

Business or Occupation Needs	9
Family Needs	1
Both	7
	17

Several legislators were apparently in the position of having to give up one of three responsibilities. The legislative responsibility was infringing upon both the family and the private business of the member. In only one case were family needs named without also naming the need to spend more time in private business. The single exception was a member whose spouse was quite ill. The findings here modify the Blair-Henry study in which greater emphasis was given to the "family" as a reason for retirement.

Dissatisfaction with recent legislative experience also may be an important factor in voluntary retirement. Seven of the forty-three respondents were explicit in this regard. Contrary to what one might expect, members who expressed this dissatisfaction were on all measures very active members of the legislature. All seven either were committee chairs or served on finance or appropriation committees. Six of seven were above the mean in their chamber party in: (1) the quantity of legislation sponsored which passed the chamber, and (2) the percent of legislation sponsored which passed the chamber. Six of the seven were majority party members. Confirmation of their dissatisfaction is noted in their responses to a separate item in which they were asked to rate on a five point scale how "rewarding" they found their last term of service. The following representation illustrates the difference between these dissatisfied members and their retiring colleagues:

		1	Very Rewarding
$(N = 34)$ Most Retirees	$x = 1.97$	2	Usually Rewarding
		3	Rewarding only part of the time
$(N = 7)$ Dissatisfied Retirees	$x = 3.27$	4	Usually not rewarding
		5	Not rewarding at all

In sum, the members who indicated dissatisfaction with their legislative experience as a reason for retiring were distinct from other retirees on a Likert-type scale item as well. These dissatisfied respondents appeared to be active and potentially influential members of their chamber. In addition, none of them indicated that they had retired to run for another office. Several of these members indicated that they were either frustrated by their experience or "burned out." A contributing factor in a majority of cases was also the member's need to spend more time in his or her business or occupation.

In a third important group are those legislators whose *career ambitions* lead them to vacate their seat to run for another office. Almost half of those who left voluntarily (21 of 43) immediately sought another office. In addition, members may accept other types of career positions in public life, such as in the state or federal bureaucracy, or the state or federal judiciary. Two members in our sample accepted appointments in federal agencies. Among those seeking elective office, several were house members seeking a senate seat. Others ran for Congress, and in some cases a local office was sought. Four of our six women respondents in this survey left to run for another office.

Of those twenty-one members who sought another office, fifteen offered no other reason for vacating their seat. Eight of the respondents wanted to move to the state senate, and others obviously wanted higher office to satisfy their career ambitions. Five of the six who gave more complex responses indicated that they needed to spend more time in their business or occupation (the sixth mentioned health). At least three of these six ran for local office (two for prosecuting attorney), and one ran for Congress. The member who ran for Congress gave a succinct explanation for his decision:

> Thus the decision was made to run for Congress and either "get in" full time in politics if I won, or "get out" if I lost and devote "full-time" to my business.

As we could have predicted from Hain's career study, those who left to run for another office were a younger group than those who left for other reasons—a mean of forty-two years of age as compared to fifty-three. By the evidence in the official records, most of those who vacated their seat to run for another office did not appear well integrated into the formal power structure of their chamber. None of the four majority party senators held a committee chairmanship in 1981, and only one served on a committee dealing with taxation, appropriations, or budget. The three house members from Indiana also did not serve on the "money" committees, nor did the single majority member hold a committee chairmanship. Only in the 163-member Missouri house did those seeking another office appear in this respect to be typical of the chamber as a whole. Members who are seeking another office may in fact avoid heavy responsibilities in their chamber in order to devote more time to building a campaign.

The progressive ambitions of members in this study may be demonstrated more clearly by their bill sponsorship activity. They may sponsor a higher volume of successful bills than those who merely sought reelection to their own seats. To make this comparison, the data (taken from the official legislative journals and indexes) were broken down by state, chamber, and party—for three reasons. First, the states have different rules for processing legislation. Second, members in the smaller senates tend to sponsor more bills (mean number of sponsorships among senators is 25.7 for Indiana and 15.1 for Missouri, whereas for House members it is 11.7 and 6.1 respectively). Finally, majority party members tend to have greater success with their legislation. For example, the mean sponsorship success rate for getting bills through the chamber was 34 percent for majority members in the two states, but only 19 percent for minority party members. The pattern holds for all four chambers. This process of sorting by state, chamber, and party status produces eight subgroups.

Within each subgroup it is possible to compare the success of bills of those who sought reelection with the success of those who sought another office. Because of the small number of cases in the latter group, the results need to be combined in some way to gain statistical confidence. We ask whether members seeking another office were above or below the mean of the reelection seekers in their subgroup. We find that in two-thirds of the cases (14 of 21) those seeking another office did sponsor more successful bills than the mean rate of the reelection seekers in their respective subgroups. This tendency will require further confirmation, but it is apparent that those seeking other offices were active in sponsoring legislation and were at least as successful as those who continued on in their legislative chamber.

In addition to legislators who retire because of opportunity costs, or dissatisfaction with the legislature, or progressive ambitions, there are those who have *health* problems or who reach what they consider to be normal *retirement age*. Seven of the forty-three respondents indicated that at least one of these factors was a consideration in their retirement from the legislature. As expected, most of these members were in an advanced age group. These personal reasons seem theoretically uninteresting, but they do constitute a part of legislative turnover.

In a final residual group, four legislators indicated that they did not run again at least partly because of *electoral expectations*, that is, because of adverse political circumstances in their districts. With only four cases, an evaluation is not appropriate, but it would seem that these legislators might be similar to those members who ran again but lost in the primary. The four members in this category apparently predicted they might lose and therefore did not run. Other members probably would not have run had they thought they would not win.

To summarize, legislators who voluntarily vacate their seats do so for a variety of reasons, the most common of which are: (1) the opportunity costs associated with their private occupation and (2) the prospects for career advancement in public office. Important also are opportunity costs associated with the family, dissatisfaction with legislative experience, health or age related considerations, and electoral expectations. The frequency of response offered in each of these categories is illustrated in Table 6.1.

A degree of caution needs to be taken when interpreting the results. While the question posed to each respondent offered a balance of options, it is nevertheless possible that some respondents were reluctant to indicate the full range of their reasons. Dissatisfaction with legislative service, for example, may be more common among respondents than has been shown. In addition, those who indicated only that they sought another office may have had reasons for doing so that were not revealed. Finally, at least some of the nonrespondents may have had more personal reasons for retiring, such as those that were found in the full sample study of Blair and Henry.

In conclusion, this analysis has shown that legislative turnover across the nation at the state level has continued to decline, but that still about 70 percent of the turnover in our selected states (Indiana and Missouri) is due to voluntary retirement. Approximately 21 percent of those legislators who were up for reelection did not run for the same seat (either in the primary or general election). Our sample suggests that about 10 percent ran for another office and that the other 10 or 11 percent chose to return to private status. Only about 8 percent of those whose seats were up for reelection actually lost the seat at the polls. A few (four in our sample) vacated their seats to avoid a possible loss.

In his study of risk-bearing and progressive ambition in Congress, Rohde (1979) was able to assume that returning to private status is an undesirable alternative except in very unusual circumstances. Historically, the return to private status has been a more viable option for state legislators. This study details some of the reasons and their significance. In recent years state legislatures have been changing from part-time to

Table 6.1 Summary of Reasons for Voluntarily Vacating Legislative Seat (N = 43)*

	Indiana	**Missouri**	**Total**
Opportunity Costs			*17 (40%)*
Occupational	7	9	16 (37%)
Family	3	5	8 (19%)
Legislative Dissatisfaction	5	2	*7 (16%)*
Career Ambitions (Public Office)			*23 (53%)*
Elective Office	5	16	21 (49%)
Other	1	1	2 (5%)
Health or Age	3	4	*7 (16%)*
Electoral Expectations	1	3	*4 (9%)*

*Percentages represent proportion of respondents who gave each response. A respondent could give more than one response.

full-time duty—meeting every year in longer sessions and in special sessions. The states are in different stages in this evolution. Future analysis would benefit by contrasting those that assume full-time duty with those that are strictly part-time. Indiana and Missouri are in the middle of this distribution. We would expect that the nature of voluntary retirement would be a reflection of those incentives that attract members to the legislature in the first place.

As legislative service becomes more demanding of members' time, we would expect fewer legislators with lucrative private occupations to make a bid for a seat, unless, of course, there is a marked increase in legislative compensation. The increase in time demands make it more likely that candidates will see themselves as full-time professionals rather than part-time citizens. Incentives to institutionalize the committee and leadership structure become more attractive. Members may have aspirations for higher office, but a career in the legislature can be made appealing also. It is in the interest of members with long-term interests in public office to improve their options.

The three major options or alternatives confronted by legislators are:

a_1 Run again for the same office

a_2 Run for a "higher" office

a_3 Retire from office (returning to private status)

The decision of each legislator will depend on the expected utility of each option. Borrowing from the formalization of Rohde (1979; also see Riker and Ordeshook, 1973, ch. 3), the *expected utility* of each option may be stated as follows:

$$E(a_1) = P_1(O_1) \, U(O_1) - C(a_1)$$

$$E(a_2) = P_2(O_2) \, U(O_2) - C(a_2)$$

$$E(a_3) = U(O_3) - C(a_3)$$

where P_i is the probability that outcome j will occur if alternative i is selected, $U(O_j)$ is the utility to the legislators if outcome j is selected, $C(a_i)$ is the direct utility cost of selecting alternative i, and O_1, O_2, and O_3 are the outcomes corresponding to the listed alternatives.

The above equations assume that a legislator must give up one office to run for another and that $P = 1.0$. Generally, we would expect that the probability of winning a higher office is substantially less than that of winning reelection to the same seat, thus even though the potential benefits derived from higher office are greater, they are usually more than offset by the low probability of winning. In the two-state study there were 304 seats on the line. Approximately 79 percent of the incumbents chose alternative a_1, and only about 8 percent did not succeed in regaining their seats. Alternatives a_2 and a_3 were selected with about equal frequency by the other incumbents. Thus when chances are four out of five that legislators will seek reelection, the desire to build up the attractiveness of continued service is likely to be widespread. Institutionalization of the committee system is one way to do it.

It is in the self-interest of members to create a committee system that distributes widely the benefits to be had in the form of legislation. In some instances this will mean nothing more than claiming credit for legislation to satisfy constituents who may be influential in the next election. In other cases, ideological differences may be at stake. In any case, the situation is far different than it was at the turn of the century, when legislators had a very limited interest in state legislative service.

Thus in spite of the dissatisfaction that may be created by excessive numbers of workdays in the state capitols (as implied by the findings in chapter 5), 80 percent of the legislators choose nevertheless to seek reelection to the same seat. With a 90 percent chance of success, such as in Indiana or Missouri, other options become less attractive. In this respect the state legislative incentive system is becoming much more like that of Congress. As legislators see the prospect of a career, they are more likely to want the institutionalization of incentives in the conduct of official business. Chair and committee assignments take on added importance. They are likely to want visible benefits in the form of legislation, and time away from the state capitol may be valued more for shoring up political support, as in the case of members of Congress (e.g., see Parker, 1986), than for outside business or personal activities. Even now many state legislators maintain offices in their districts, and such a phenomenon may be the next wave in state legislative elaboration of the office.

Part Three

Explorations in Efficiency and Reform

7

Risk, Efficiency, and Adaptation in Committee Decision Making

Committees are created in a variety of ways. Perhaps the most interesting from a purely philosophical perspective is the *voluntary* self-selected committee that forms without any jurisdictional, organizational, or membership restrictions. In more structured situations, however, such as those considered in this work, committee formation usually involves *delegations* of responsibility or authority. Such actions may be divided into two main categories:

1. Those in which one person delegates decision making to a few, or a few delegate to many.
2. Those in which many delegate decision making to a few (or to one).

In this book it is the latter of these two types of action that is of primary concern. Nevertheless, it will be helpful to consider briefly delegations to larger groups.

Delegating from One to Few or Few to Many

By definition, a committee arrives at decisions through voting or the counting of preferences. Thus the question of why a purely voluntary committee forms is really a question of why individuals choose to abide

by a voting rule. The latter question in turn raises a number of fundamental choices that pit the use of a voting rule against alternative ways
of achieving goals. The alternatives include direct bargaining, the use or
threat of force, delegation of responsibility to an individual or group
that is not a committee, or simply autonomous individual action or inaction. When an individual chooses to abide by a voting rule, he or she in
essence delegates individual discretion to committee rule (i.e., from one
to many). Motivations for participating voluntarily in committee decision making are similar to those elicited in an institutional context.

The delegation of decision making to a larger number of participants may seem the reverse of what legislators normally do, but it is an
important option for most committee systems. Most of the states in the
U.S., for example, have constitutional provisions that allow the legislature to use a voluntary referendum. The principal reason for individuals to expand participation in decisions is to *reduce risk*. When legislators choose to place a measure on the ballot (assuming it is not
constitutionally required), it is usually to avoid the electoral risks of a
legislative stalemate or the consequences of taking an unpopular position. Revenue and tax matters are frequent subjects of such procedures.

Risk. There are several specific risk-related reasons for enlarging
the committee decision-making setting. In settings where deliberation is
possible, a larger group may supply either additional alternatives, or
more complete information regarding the consequences of various alternatives. Even where the quality of the information pool is not expected
to increase, the referral of decisions to larger committees may have a
symbolic advantage and help legitimize the decisions. Even when neither of the above advantages is apparent, delegating the decisions will
buy additional time and perhaps cause a needed delay in the settlement
of issues. Finally, given that the decisions may carry negative consequences of some magnitude, it may be appealing to shift or spread the
risk. Legislators are noted for wanting to claim credit. They are not
noted for wanting to take the blame. Nor are most other humans.

In most legislative committee systems, the need to reduce risk and
delegate decisions to larger committees is satisfied by constitutional
requirements or official legislative procedures. The full standing committee passes judgment on legislation forwarded by its subcommittees.
Legislative proposals surviving the standing committee must be approved by a majority of the entire chamber in order to pass. In addition,
a second chamber often rules on the legislation approved by the first

chamber. Within these general guidelines, legislatures do vary somewhat in their practices.

Most American legislatures allow committees the autonomy to sit on proposals indefinitely, although in a few states the committees are required to report out all legislation, with or without a favorable recommendation. In many states the party caucus is active and will pass judgment upon legislation considered by committees. In contrast, in many other states the party caucus seldom meets. In the parliaments of many nations, the standing or select committees are confined to the details of legislation. In the U.S., the standing committees are often the architects of legislation. These differences, however, should not overshadow the fact that risk reduction is a principal concern in any committee system.

Adaptation. The management of risk occurs in several different ways. A primary organizational means of managing risk is to make all major decisions subject to multiple review. When review procedures become standard practice, individuals in the organization will learn to take precautionary or anticipatory action. In a committee system such reviews are concluded in a committee vote. Thus the best way for a member to anticipate the action of a review committee is to poll its membership. A poll is a simulated vote.

Among seasoned observers of legislative politics, it is conventional wisdom that sophisticated legislators prefer to reduce the risk of defeat in a larger forum by first initiating polls of membership opinion. The party whips are best known for this function, but in American legislatures, where standing committees are strong, the committee chair and bill sponsors are often the poll takers. It is also common for lobbyists and newspapers to take their own polls. Obviously poll taking takes time and energy, and there is a limit to how much of it can be done.

Delegating from Many to Few

The central reason for delegating decision making to a smaller group or committee is to reduce the amount of time and energy it takes to arrive at decisions. The *decision costs* per member are reduced by initiating a *division of labor* and *economies of scale*. In the simplest of situations, the larger group assigns one or more tasks to a single committee that is composed of fewer members. The smaller committee is asked to specialize and to act according to one of the following guidelines:

1. Act with complete autonomy.

2. Ask for approval from the larger group for any decision that causes a change in the status quo.

3. Ask for approval from the larger group for all decisions.

The first alternative represents the most complete division of labor, since nonmembers of the smaller committee have no further responsibility for the tasks of the smaller committee. The second alternative is a halfway house, requiring approval from the parent group on decisions that create change—but on decisions to delay or block, only members who are on the small committee participate. The third and last alternative above represents a division of labor only in the sense that the members of the small committee may go into greater detail than those not on the committee.

Most American legislatures adopt the second guideline. The standing committees report back to the chamber only those legislative measures they approve. For the typical member the workload decreases from a consideration of all proposals to a consideration of proposals that are:

1. Assigned to the member's standing committees

2. Reported to the floor from other committees

3. Not in the above but on the member's personal agenda

To illustrate, assume a one-hundred-member chamber with one thousand proposals and twenty committees. A particular member has introduced ten bills and serves on three committees which together receive 150 (3/20) bills. Forty percent of all proposals in other committees reach the floor. The member must consider 150 bills in his three committees, plus 340 of the 850 bills in other committees, plus a small number of personal bills (e.g., 3 or 4) not included previously. In sum, the member must consider only slightly less than 50 percent of the legislation. The percentage would be reduced even further if each committee employed subcommittees.

The Decision versus External Cost Dilemma

Whenever a decision is made to reduce decision costs by reducing the number who must approve a decision, there is risk of increasing external costs (adverse repercussions). Buchanan and Tullock, in *The Cal-*

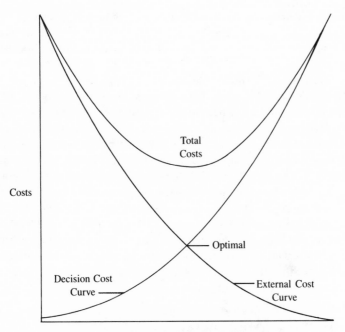

Fig. 7.1 Theoretical Relationship between Decision Costs and External Costs

culus of Consent (1962), explore the nature of this dilemma and suggest that there may be some optimal level of approval that would minimize the sum of these costs. Buchanan and Tullock were concerned with broad questions of constitutional decision making; nevertheless, their thesis might be helpful if revised and refined to apply to legislative institutions. They distinguish between *private decision costs*, as illustrated above in our division of labor example, and *interpersonal decision costs*, which are decreased through economies of scale. They speculate that there is a *direct* curvilinear relationship between interpersonal decision costs and the number who must approve a proposal. In other words, in a group of fixed size, an increase in the fraction of members required for approval will lead to increases in interpersonal decision costs at an increasing rate. Reaching agreement becomes increasingly difficult as those who are less in agreement with a proposal must be added to form a winning coalition.

Buchanan and Tullock would suggest, however, an *inverse* curvilinear relationship between external costs and the number who must approve. As the fraction who approve is increased, the external costs or adverse repercussions that will occur will decrease at a decreasing rate.

Buchanan and Tullock did not go into sufficient detail to explain why the above relationships are curvilinear. Greater discussion of these expectations will be taken up in the next chapter in relation to the specific aspects of legislative organization. Here it is sufficient to observe that when the two cost curves are curvilinear, one positive and one negative, and if in theory the costs are additive, then the curves can be combined to produce Figure 7.1; the figure illustrates an optimal point. On the graph, the point at which these two cost curves intersect would indicate an optimal approval level (total costs would be minimized). As the number who must approve is increased beyond the optimal level, for example, decision costs accelerate and external costs decline, but at a slower rate. The parabola represents the sum of decision and external costs at each point.

Problems in Application

There are a number of problems with the above thesis as it applies to legislatures. First of all, private decision costs—obtaining information about legislative proposals and making up one's mind—are a very important part of a legislative day. For example, in the survey of legislators of fifty states, the *private* decision costs, as measured by amount of time spent obtaining and understanding information about bills (first item in Table 7.1), were equal to the total of *interpersonal* time costs, which included finding out how other members felt about the issues and hammering out compromises (second and third items in Table 7.1).

A second problem in applying the Buchanan-Tullock thesis arises from the notion that external costs result only from decisions made. External costs can result also from decisions not made. Thus while it may seem to make sense to have large standing committees in legislatures to achieve greater representation and approval before sending legislation to the floor, such large committees may act sluggishly and suppress demands for action. These counteracting influences may be understood partly through the notion of *risk*. Legislators must weigh two types of risk: (1) the risk of making a change; and (2) the risk of maintaining the status quo. External costs can result from either choice.

Table 7.1 Committee Work Distributions in a Typical Legislative Day (in Hours)

Q. Of those hours you spend on committee-subcommittee work, how would you estimate they are allocated among the following activities?

Type of Activity	All Members	Majority Members	Minority Members
Obtaining information about proposals in order to understand their content.	1.96	1.97	1.93
Finding out how other members feel about the issues (formal and informal discussions).	.82	.87	.72
Hammering out workable compromises with members of the committee(s).	1.10	1.13	1.02
Reviewing conduct of administrative agencies.	.50	.52	.46
Other committee work.	.24	.24	.25
Totals	4.62	4.73	4.38

a. Range of n = 1714–1923
b. Range of n = 1116–1221
c. Range of n = 598–672

A third problem in the application of the decision cost and external cost theme arises from the complexity of legislative committee organization. In other words, we cannot examine simply a single standing committee out of context and determine, say, its optimal membership size. Several other factors may have a bearing upon its optimal form, including the size of the legislative chamber itself, and the extent to which the committee utilizes subcommittees. The amount of legislation received by a committee should have a bearing also. Optimal committee size makes less sense than the notion of optimal committee system (or systems). These optimalities are explored in chapter 8.

A fourth problem in applying the above thesis is that most American legislatures labor under the condition of excess demand for action. The demands for time and action are likely to exceed greatly the capacity of the committee system to supply well-informed responses to all such demands. Under this condition, legislators have two organizational alternatives to attempt to meet the demand. The first is to increase the number of legislative workdays, either by mutual agreement or constitutional amendment. The second is to improve the internal structure (committee organization, staffing, etc.) and rules for making decisions. The first alternative offers an increase in decision costs in exchange for additional benefits in outcomes. The results in chapter 6 would suggest that in practice such a solution falls far short of being Pareto-optimal. Many legislators would anticipate substantial increases in opportunity costs. Legislators who experienced more workdays tended to be less satisfied with the product of their efforts.

The second alternative, improving the internal structure, offers lower decision costs per item of business, but it probably will not affect total decision costs because of excess demand for action. In other words, efficiency advancements must be measured not in total decision costs but in improved outcomes.

Adaptation

When the risks of taking action are too high or the costs of inefficiency too burdensome, we would expect individuals to initiate some type of adaptive behavior. As mentioned earlier, to cut down on risk, legislators frequently will poll the views of members prior to taking formal action on legislation. To reduce decision costs, legislators have a number of alternatives. If they receive too many committee assignments, or if the committees are too large to work effectively, legislators may begin to miss meetings on a selective basis. If legislators are unable to evaluate thoroughly all the legislation that they must vote up or down, they may choose to ignore proposals of lesser personal value. Alternatively, they may find shortcuts for arriving at positions such as asking the opinion of a trusted expert or friend, or by respecting the wishes of the committee chair. The costs of information might be reduced also by ignoring minority party members' views, and legislators may choose not to bargain over legislation except in small subcommittees. Thus, there is a variety of individual and informal ways that legislators can employ to better accomplish their goals.

Legislatures have a formal structure and formal rules, the exact nature of which may have an impact upon the ability of legislators to achieve their goals. Inefficiencies may be remedied by changing the formal structure and rules, but if there is insufficient agreement as to what is necessary, legislators may very well improve their conditions by adapting their behavior in response to their particular circumstances.

Because of individual and informal adaptive behavior, formal organizational differences in legislatures will not have the impact that might be expected. Nevertheless, if conditions continue to worsen, as when the number of committees and committee assignments continues to expand in response to leadership incentives to hand out patronage, the members may institute a major reorganization of operating rules. The following chapters include specific consideration of formal and informal adaptive behavior.

8

Committee System Optimalities: Size Preferences and Member Adaptation

In the previous chapter the "costs of decision making" were classified into two types: (1) Decision Costs, and (2) External Costs. Decision costs are incurred as a positive curvilinear function of the fraction of membership required for approval, whereas external costs, following Buchanan and Tullock, are a negative curvilinear function of that fraction. Given these assumptions, it makes sense to ask how they might be applied to a legislative institution. In the last chapter a number of conceptual problems with this approach were discussed. In this chapter an empirical investigation will offer more specific modifications. In particular, how can decision costs and external costs be evaluated in relation to committees, committee size, and the structure of the committee system?

The analysis to follow demonstrates that in a legislative setting it makes more sense to develop the notion of "optimal committee system" rather than optimal committee size. Evidence is provided also to suggest that legislators do adapt in predictable ways to "inefficiencies" in committee organization, but that it is not possible in all circumstances for them to compensate.

A Theoretical Model for a Single Committee

Earlier theoretical work has established the significance of "decision rules" for evaluating costs and benefits of decision making (Rae, 1969). Legislative committees, however, almost universally employ majority rule, not two-thirds, three-fourths, and so forth. The number who must approve a proposal is therefore a direct function of committee size. Thus we may hypothesize that an increase in committee size will lead to:

1. a rate increase in decision costs
2. a rate decrease in external costs

More formally, these relationships may be expressed as:

$$D = f\{N^g\} \qquad\qquad 8.1$$

$$E = f\{N^{-k}\} \qquad\qquad 8.2$$

where D refers to Decision Costs, E to External Costs, N to the number of members on the committee, and where $g > 1$ and $-k < -1$ to signify the expectation that the relationships are curvilinear.

The first equation suggests that, other things being equal (such as the voting rule, and the right of members to speak and bargain), decision costs will increase at a faster rate than membership size. The accelerating factor in this relationship is found in the complexities of bargaining. The number of bargaining combinations and corresponding coalition possibilities expands very rapidly—as a factorial of the number of committee members.

The second equation above suggests that as committee size increases, external costs decrease at an even faster rate. A committee majority becomes very quickly a more representative sample of its parent majority as the size of the committee is increased—much in the way random samples work. The larger the committee, the less it can be oriented toward special interests, and hence the less it suffers from the repercussions of special interest decisions.

The goal of the individual legislator is to *minimize $D + E$*. If we assume that the above is a plausible portrayal of the effects of committee size, it may be shown, using standard minimizing procedures, that for each legislator there is an optimal committee size. Letting $C = D + E$, we may sum the two cost equations such that:

$$C = f\{N^g + N^{-k}\} \qquad\qquad 8.3$$

Taking the first derivative to minimize total costs with respect to committee size (N), we find

$$dC/dN = gN^{(g-1)} + kN^{(-k-1)} = 0$$

which reduces to:

$$N^{(g+k)} = k/g$$

$$N = e^{(1/g+k)(\ln(k/g))} \quad \text{where } N \text{ is optimal.} \qquad 8.4$$

These equations simply confirm the existence of an optimal committee size as a result of summing the cost equations. As pointed out by Buchanan and Tullock (1962), total costs will take on a parabolic shape (Figure 8.1), the lowest point of which is optimal.

How plausible is this model? It does not suggest that the optimal committee size is the same for all members, nor that individuals will have the same tolerances for decision costs or external costs. Many

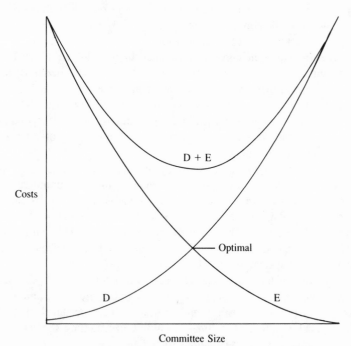

Fig. 8.1 Decision/External Cost Functions for Varying Committee Sizes under Constant Decision Rule

other factors, such as the use of subcommittees, the role of the chair, and the motivations of members serving in the legislative body, would need to be taken into account.

Also, in chapter 7 decision costs were divided into "private" decision costs and "interpersonal" decision costs. Private decision costs are a direct function of the number of proposals. Interpersonal decision costs are probably a function of both the number of proposals and the number of members. Equations 8.1 and 8.3 are thus incomplete unless it is assumed that the number of proposals is a constant. Several of these modifications will be taken up later. The present task is to make a simple test of the model.

An Empirical Test

The direct measurement of decision costs and external costs is a complex and messy business, but there is a different way to get at the problem and thereby indirectly test the illustrated model. In a nationwide sample of state legislators, the following question was posed:

> From your experience in committee work, what would you regard as the *ideal* committee size (# of members) for the following type of committee?
> ——— a typical standing committee of your chamber

This item was first administered to a sample of 511 state legislators after the 1979 legislative sessions in each state. The results are reported by the author in a 1982 article. This analysis utilizes the later and more complete returns of a 1981 survey of two thousand state legislators.

We might surmise that there would be an equilibrium factor at work in the responses to the above question. When a member feels that the standing committees are larger than optimal size, he or she may indicate a preference for smaller committees; likewise, if the committees seem too small, a preference for larger committees may be expressed. We should not expect legislators to know the "optimal size" committee, but we would expect them to provide informed judgment about whether or not their experiences suggest that their committees have too many or too few members.

In order to make the best use of the judgments provided by legislators, two measures of *actual* committee size have been developed:

1. *Average Committee Size* (A1). Calculated from the official committee listings of each state. "Housekeeping" committees not included.

2. *Average Named-Committee Size* (A2). Legislators were asked to name two committees on which they served. The responses were verified in the records, and the sizes recorded and averaged. Cases were omitted in this analysis if only one committee was named.

The first measure is more likely to tap the entire standing committee experience of legislators in each chamber, whereas the second measure focuses upon the immediate past experience. An ample proportion of legislators served on only two standing committees.

Letting I = Ideal Committee Size for each respondent, and $A1$ and $A2$ the respective mean values of "actual" committee size, we are able to observe that the "ideal" is highly related to experience, where

$$r^2_{I(A1)} = .64 \qquad (N = 1958)$$
$$r^2_{I(A2)} = .41 \qquad (N = 1922)$$

Legislators are likely to suggest an incremental change, if any, and only rarely a fundamental alteration (at least in a survey instrument of the kind used here). Thus instead of treating the "ideal" responses as absolutes, we may treat them as *expressions of preference to move off the status quo*, such that:

$$Q1 = I - A1$$
$$Q2 = I - A2$$

where:

1. A positive Q value means a preference for larger committees.

2. A Q value of O means a preference for committees of the same size.

3. A negative Q value means a preference for smaller committees.

The Q differences allow an evaluation of the minimization model. If the model is to be retained, we should find that the relationship between Q and A is consistent with the parabolic relationship illustrated in Figure 8.1. If in fact members of committees do seek to minimize the sum of decision costs and external costs, and if in fact the costs are exponential functions of committee size, one direct and the other inverse, we should find that the responses exhibit a weighing of these costs. In

Table 8.1 Differences between Preferred and Actual Committee
Size (I–A1)

Actual Size	1981 N	Mean Values of Q (1981)	Mean Values of Q (1979)	1979 N
5–6.99	126	+.26	+.22	49
7–8.99	218	−.04	+.28	69
9–10.99	331	−.30	−.52	60
11–12.99	340	−.76	−.82	56
13–14.99	181	−1.32	−1.25	86
15–16.99	196	−1.64	−2.33	40
17–18.99	219	−1.98	−1.81	67
19–20.99	168	−2.74	−3.82	33
21–	179	−3.14	−4.11	32

Table 8.2 Differences between Preferred and Actual Committee
Size (I–A2)*

Actual Size	1981 N	Mean Values of Q (1981)	Mean Values of Q (1979)	1979 N
5–6.99	82	+.76	+.62	29
7–8.99	144	+.18	+.56	50
9–10.99	226	−.50	−.41	37
11–12.99	206	−1.00	−1.32	59
13–14.99	207	−1.94	−1.85	52
15–16.99	241	−2.58	−2.30	64
17–18.99	136	−2.81	−3.53	38
19–20.99	151	−2.99	−3.23	30
21–22.99	71	−5.62	−6.08	20
23–24.99	44	−6.84	−9.14	14
25–26.99	70	−7.86	−7.19	8
27–28.99	32	−10.08	−9.50	6
29–30.99	14	−10.21	−11.67	6
31–32.99	18	−14.33	−11.87	4
33–	25	−25.78	−24.50	7

*The figures in this table do not contain responses from members who named only one committee on which they served.

Table 8.3   Subcommittee Use and the Relationship between Actual and Preferred Committee Size

Committee Size (A2)	Extent of Subcommittee Use				Differences	
	High		Low		1981 High-Low	1979 High-Low
	Q2	N	Q2	N		
5–6.99	+.91	36	+.64	46	.27	1.42
7–8.99	+.49	57	−.02	87	.51	.56
9–10.99	−.37	141	−.69	85	.32	.67
11–12.99	−.85	151	−1.41	55	.56	.09
13–14.99	−1.84	112	−2.08	95	.24	.46
15–16.99	−2.29	169	−3.28	72	.99	.94
17–18.99	−2.82	114	−2.75	22	−.07	2.33
19–20.99	−3.17	125	−2.13	26	−1.04	7.00
21–22.99	−5.83	57	−4.79	14	−1.04	1.63
23–24.99	−6.32	36	−9.19	8	2.87	2.17
25–26.99	−7.60	66	−12.25	4	4.65	8.93
27–28.99	−10.08	32		0		
29–30.99	−10.21	14		0		
31–32.99	−14.33	18		0		10.17
33–	−25.78	25		0		6.25

other words, the responses must illustrate a tendency to move to an optimum (or equilibrium).

To illustrate, the average committee size measures (A1 and A2) may be classified into intervals of 5 to 6.99, 7 to 8.99, 9 to 10.99 . . . , to cover the entire range for ninety-nine chambers. In each category of committee size, the differences in preference (Q values) can be averaged, yielding the results illustrated in Tables 8.1 and 8.2. As may be observed, members of standing committees with small memberships do tend to prefer somewhat larger committees (e.g., $Q1 = +.26$, $Q2 = +.76$) than they experience. Members from committees with larger memberships tend to prefer smaller committees. The responses are consistent with the theoretical model. In the more extended classification in Table 8.2, it is more apparent that as committee size increases beyond a membership of nine, legislators prefer even greater percentage reductions in committee size. The relationship is curvilinear as mapped in Figure 8.1.

Do the above results mean that for the "typical" legislator the optimal standing committee size is between seven and nine? Not necessarily. It is possible that the overall result reflects the averaging of different situation-specific optima.

The Subcommittee Effect

As one possible modification, we may hypothesize that *the use of subcommittees will tend to reduce total costs, primarily by reducing decision costs*. A further division of labor into subcommittees could reduce the number of proposals members would consider and might reduce the number of active participants in the bargaining process over particular legislative measures. If this is the case, we should find that when subcommittees are employed, legislators will be satisfied with somewhat larger standing committees. If they are more satisfied, the differences should surface in a comparison of legislators working under *high* and *low* subcommittee use. The 1981 fifty-state survey allows us to make

Table 8.4 Large and Small Chamber and the Relationship between Actual and Preferred Committee Size (1981)

Committee Size (A2)	Size of Legislative Chamber					Differences (Large – Small)
	80+			<80		
	(Q2)	N		(Q2)	N	
5–6.99		0		+.76	82	
7–8.99	+3.12	12		−.09	132	3.21
9–10.99	+.14	33		−.61	193	.75
11–12.99	−.03	77		−1.57	129	1.54
13–14.99	−1.22	78		−2.39	129	1.17
15–16.99	−2.26	102		−2.82	139	.56
17–18.99	−2.87	103		−2.61	33	−.26
19–20.99	−2.47	131		−6.40	20	3.93
21–22.99	−5.56	64		−6.21	7	.77
23–24.99	−6.60	43		−17.00	1	10.40
25–26.99	−6.37	59		−15.86	11	9.49
27–28.99	−9.16	29		−19.00	3	9.84
29–30.99	−10.25	12		−9.95	2	−.35
31–32.99	−14.47	17		−12.00	1	−2.47
33–	−25.78	25			0	

this distinction. Those classified in the "high" group indicated that sub-committees were a part of their official chamber rules and/or used on a regular basis by many committees. Approximately two-thirds of the respondents were in this high use group. The remaining respondents, those in the "lower" use group, indicated that subcommittees were not used very often or that they were not used at all.

An examination of Table 8.3 reveals that for most size categories of standing committee (and in all categories where $N > 30$), legislators experiencing high subcommittee use prefer larger committees (see "high-low" column). The 1981 data are consistent with the 1979 data in this respect. In addition, the optimal committee size, as suggested by the change in signs from $+$ to $-$, appears to be approximately *nine* for the high use group and closer to *seven* for the low use group. Finally, it should be noted that there are very few cases in the sample where those serving on committees of seventeen or more also report low subcommittee use. Legislators almost always resort to subcommittees when the committees get too large or too busy.

The Chamber Size Effect

As a second modification, we may hypothesize that *larger chambers lead to the creation of larger standing committees, perhaps to reduce external costs of such committees.* If this is the case, we should find that legislators from larger chambers will actually prefer larger committees than will those legislators from smaller chambers. To make this test in an illustrative manner, the respondents from the 1981 survey may be divided into those who are from:

1. Chambers where membership is less than 80. Includes all state senates and 12 state houses. $N = 882$.

2. Chambers where membership is 80 or greater. Includes 37 state houses. $N = 785$.

Using the differences between actual and preferred committee sizes as before, it may be seen in Table 8.4 (last column) that in larger chambers legislators do in fact find larger committees more acceptable. Also, in small chambers large committees are not used very often. Finally, the optimality estimate in large chambers is about *eleven,* whereas it is closer to seven in smaller chambers.

The combined effects of chamber size and subcommittee use is il-

Table 8.5 Chamber Size, Subcommittee Use, and the Relationship between Actual and Preferred Committee Size (1981)

Committee Membership Size (A2)	Large Chambers Subcommittee Use		Small Chambers Subcommittee Use	
	High	*Low*	*High*	*Low*
5–6.99			+.92(36)	+.64(46)
7–8.99	+4.92(6)	+1.33(6)	−.03(51)	−.13(81)
9–10.99	+.48(26)	−1.14(7)	−.57(115)	−.65(78)
11–12.99	+.12(63)	−.71(14)	−1.55(88)	−1.65(41)
13–14.99	−1.46(54)	−.69(24)	−2.19(58)	−2.55(71)
15–16.99	−2.18(76)	−2.50(26)	−2.38(93)	−3.73(46)
17–18.99	−2.89(83)	−2.78(20)	−2.61(31)	−2.50(2)
19–20.99	−2.57(106)	−2.06(25)	−6.52(19)	−4.00(1)
21–22.99	−5.86(51)	−4.38(13)	−5.58(6)	−10.00(1)
23–24.99	−6.01(35)	−9.19(8)	−17.00(1)	
25–26.99	−6.16(56)	−10.33(3)	−15.65(10)	−18.00(1)
27–28.99	−9.16(29)		−19.00(3)	
29–30.99	−10.25(12)		−9.95(2)	
31–32.99	−14.47(17)			
33–	−25.78(25)			

Number of cases enclosed in parentheses.

lustrated in Table 8.5. In large chambers that experience high subcommittee use the optimal committee size estimate moves upward to *between twelve and thirteen*—as opposed to approximately *nine* where there is low subcommittee use. In small chambers (80 or less), however, the use of subcommittees seems to make very little difference in the response patterns. At this point it pays to note that subcommittees may not be used in state legislatures in the manner to which we are accustomed when observing the U.S. Congress. In the states, subcommittees frequently have very little autonomy, and the full committee very often conducts full hearings and duplicates the work of the subcommittees. The subcommittee's role may be little more than one of taking responsibility for the discussion when the full committee meets to consider the legislation seriously. These circumstances would seem to be more prevalent in smaller chambers where members tend to have many more committee assignments and where subcommittees act more informally.

The crux of the above analysis is to suggest that while the notion of optimal committee size has some merit, it makes more sense to pursue the notions of optimal committee systems or optimal decision-making conditions. Legislator preferences will vary with legislative structure.

Structural and Behavioral Adaptation

If we can assume that legislators have in mind the purpose of minimizing total costs (decision plus external), then it can be expected that they will adjust to possible "inefficiencies" in the committee system. One obvious way to make this adjustment is to do it formally by altering the organizational structure. The previous analysis of optimalities brought together three structural features: (1) chamber size; (2) committee size; and (3) subcommittee use. If we examine the ninety-nine state chambers we find that chamber size does in fact influence average committee size, and that average committee size in turn influences the degree of subcommittee use, such that:

$$\begin{array}{c} [\text{CHAMBER SIZE}] \\ \downarrow {\scriptstyle .65} \\ [\text{AVERAGE COMMITTEE SIZE}] \\ \downarrow {\scriptstyle .43} \\ [\text{SUBCOMMITTEE USE}] \end{array}$$

where the relationship between chamber size and subcommittee use is spurious (Francis and Riddlesperger, 1982).

In earlier chapters, we saw that legislative leaders and followers alike prefer standing committees in order to process the agenda more efficiently than would be possible in full forum. In the language of this chapter, the use of committees has the property of reducing decision costs per item of business and of reducing the *status quo* external costs that could result from inaction. By way of refinement, we learn here that legislators in chambers with large memberships create larger standing committees. This creation of larger committees occurs in part no doubt simply because there are more members to place on committees, but perhaps also in part because there is need to reduce the external costs of those committee members and to minimize problems on the floor. A larger standing committee is needed in a larger chamber in order to reduce risk of defeat by maintaining sufficient representation of the full membership.

Just as a large chamber needs committees to process the agenda efficiently, a large standing committee may need subcommittees. Legislators adapt to the situation at hand by altering the structure, often on an ad hoc basis, but frequently by formal rule or policy. Whether any particular standing committee actually utilizes subcommittees may depend in part on how many proposals it receives. A large committee with nothing to do has little need for subcommittees.

Those problems not accommodated by changes in the formal structure may be resolved nevertheless by further adaptation in individual behavior. One obvious way to adjust to committees that are too large is selectively to miss their meetings. If the tactic of missing meetings is widely practiced, then those meetings will be conducted with fewer members, and the problem of excessive decision costs is reduced. Such a practice is most likely to occur when the leadership has given members too many committee assignments. In other words, the committees are either too large, too numerous, or both.

Committee attendance is a phenomenon difficult to measure on a broad scale. Accurate records usually are not kept and members drop in and out of meetings as the situation requires. In the nationwide survey of American states, legislators were asked a series of questions about two committees on which they served. In addition to many other items they were asked:

How many members were typically present at a committee meeting? A _____ B _____

where A and B referred back to the two committees the legislators named. These answers then were matched with the actual memberships determined by checking the official records.

The first column in Table 8.6 illustrates that as committee size increases, estimates of attendance decrease, from approximately 100 percent attendance in the smallest committees to approximately 70 percent attendance in committees of twenty-three members or more. Attendance rates appear to fluctuate around 70 percent once the standing committees reach a particular size. The decline in attendance appears to be a function of committee size. A series of regression experiments were implemented to include other variables, including majority party percent, number of committee assignments, subcommittee use, and estimated frequency of meetings. None of these experiments diminished the significance of committee size, and none of the additional variables (as measured in this analysis) were statistically discernable in relation to committee attendance.

That committee attendance appears to level off somewhere between 65 and 70 percent is not surprising. A quorum is usually 50% + 1, and

Table 8.6 Committee Attendance: Relationship to Actual Committee
Size and Preferred Committee Size

Committee Size (A2)	Average Attendance (Estimate)		Average Difference (Ideal–Actual Attendance)	
5–6.99	100%	(77)	1.65	(119)
7–8.99	89	(138)	.97	(135)
9–10.99	85	(216)	.92	(208)
11–12.99	84	(190)	.95	(188)
13–14.99	79	(208)	1.02	(196)
15–16.99	78	(235)	.88	(230)
17–18.99	76	(129)	1.50	(126)
19–20.99	80	(141)	.94	(136)
21–22.99	80	(70)	−1.08	(67)
23–24.99	71	(46)	.24	(43)
25–26.99	63	(66)	1.39	(64)
27–28.99	71	(32)	−1.90	(30)
29–30.99	72	(12)	−2.20	(12)
31–32.99	67	(18)	−3.92	(18)
33–	69	(26)	−14.20	(23)

Number of cases enclosed in parentheses.

sometimes more, and in about one-third of the cases majority support
of the *full* committee membership is required to pass a measure. We
might surmise that committee chairs will round up ample majorities if
necessary.

Actual attendance may be considered a behavioral adjustment to
perceived or actual inefficiencies in the committee structure. Attendance
in standing committees corresponds rather closely to legislators' perceptions of "ideal" committee size, as illustrated in Table 8.6. As committee size increases, attendance drops off to more or less coincide with
expressed preferences. Only when the committee sizes are larger than
thirty or so do legislators not adjust to preferences.

The above results would seem to suggest that legislators will find
ways to adapt to deficiencies in organization, either by making structural changes or by autonomous individual behavior. It is no surprise
perhaps that humans are able to correct structural defects, nor is it really
that surprising that they are able to adjust individual behavior to make
further corrections. *Is this ability to adjust then so ingenious that real
legislative bodies all hover near optimal arrangements?* In the next sec-

tion we can take up an example of how some legislators simply endure suboptimal conditions.

Chamber Size and Joint Committees

An examination of ninety-nine legislative chambers reveals that the membership size of chambers influences both the average committee size and the number of committees created. This dual impact may be modeled such that:

$$
\underset{\text{[NUMBER OF COMMITTEES]}}{\overset{.37}{\nwarrow}} \quad \text{[CHAMBER SIZE]} \quad \underset{\text{[AVERAGE COMMITTEE SIZE]}}{\overset{.65}{\nearrow}}
$$

where the relationship between the number of committees and average committee size is spurious ($r = .20$). In other words, members or leaders in larger chambers, in order to achieve their goals, appoint more committees and larger committees. We may infer that the features of an "optimal" committee system are dependent upon chamber size.

If the size of the chamber is in fact an important factor in selecting the number and size of committees, then the puzzle will be especially perplexing for *joint* committee systems. We would expect that in complete joint committee systems, where there is also a major imbalance in the size of the house and senate chambers, the members of at least one chamber will be unhappy with the committee system. The committee systems of American state legislatures may be classified into four major groups (based on 1981 data):

Traditional. The chamber committee systems operate separately and differences are resolved in conference or informally. Some of these states do allocate minor functions to joint committees (e.g., Arizona, California, Kansas, Mississippi, New Jersey, West Virginia). All states not listed below are in this category.

Joint Committee. All or almost all committee functions are performed by joint committees. Includes Connecticut, Maine, and Massachusetts, although the latter state has separate Ways and Means, Rules, and Ethics committees.

Joint Finance. "Money bills" are processed by joint committees and/or subcommittees, while "non-money" bills and/or authorization are processed separately in each chamber. Includes Arkansas, Colorado, Delaware, South Dakota, Utah, Wisconsin, and Wyoming.

Mixed Use. Important functions are handled both in separate cham-

Table 8.7 Criticisms of Committee Systems by Senators in
Legislatures with Joint Committees and in Other
Legislatures (in Percentages)

Type of Criticism	Conn	Maine	Mass	Other Senates
Most members receive too many committee assignments.	77	27	42	19
Many committees are too large to work effectively.	30	13	14	7
For many members the schedule of meetings (committee-subcommittee) creates attendance problems.	85	67	71	49

ber committees and in joint committees, depending on subject matter.
Appropriations and finance are processed separately. Includes Maryland
and Rhode Island.

The three joint committee systems are in Connecticut, Maine and
Massachusetts; and in each case there is a great difference in the size of
the two chambers. In Connecticut there were 151 House members to 35
Senate members, in Maine 151 to 33, and in Massachusetts 160 to 40.
Each has a 4–to–1 to 5–to–1 ratio of house to senate members. Legislators from all chambers were asked to select items that they thought
characterized their committee system. Three of these items identified
problems of "procedural efficiency." We can compare the responses of
senators from the three "joint" committee states with the senate aver-
ages from all other states in Table 8.7.

As may be seen, a much higher percentage of senators from the
three "joint" committee systems register complaints. Complaints are
more frequent regarding: (1) the number of committee assignments;
(2) the size of committees; and (3) the scheduling of committee meetings. In the house chambers of these states, the members were also quite
aware of the scheduling and attendance problems, with the complaint
percentages ranging between 67 and 91, compared to 41 percent for all
other house chambers. In other states using joint committees the problem is less noticeable, partly because much of the business is handled in
the separate chambers, and partly due to the greater balance in house
and senate membership numbers.

The above example illustrates that structural problems relating to
legislative committees are not always remedied by adaptive behavior in

session decision making. Differences in chamber size call for differences in standing committee size and numbers of committees. But joint committees mean that each member of the legislature, senate or house, will serve on committees of the same size, and that together they will service the same number of committees. The negative responses of legislators in reaction to this dilemma confirms the importance of chamber size in developing the notion of optimal committee system.

9

Representation and the Reduction of Complexity in Lawmaking

Any legislature that allows all members to offer formal proposals, unlimited in number or in content, may be called an *open-input* system. Requirements that proposals must be filed by a certain date during the session, or even that they be prefiled, may reduce the actual number of proposals, but nevertheless all members have fair warning and are free to submit as much legislation as they wish. Under such a system legislators are free to sponsor legislation emanating from a variety of sources—nationwide or statewide interest groups, government agencies, constituency interest groups, private individuals, or model legislation initiated in other political systems. The same legislators, perhaps with the help of legislative staff, may initiate a variety of legislative measures of personal interest as well.

It can be argued that "open-input" is a necessary if not sufficient requirement for adequate representation. When all elected members of the legislative body can influence to some extent the content of the agenda, the suppression of diverse demands are minimized. The concept of representation goes well beyond what is directly relevant to this point (e.g., see Pitkin, 1967; Eulau, 1978; Wahlke, 1978; Jewell, 1982); it is sufficient to note that rules affecting the agenda are crucial. Under an open-input system, constituents have the opportunity to organize and express their demands in the form of legislative proposals–they need only a sponsor. And legislators can decide whether such proposals allow them to better represent their constituency.

Because American legislatures, with rare exception, are open-input systems,[1] they are faced with an extraordinary level of demand for action (Rosenthal and Forth, 1978; Francis, 1985b). Each chamber initiates hundreds if not thousands of proposals each legislative session. The great volume of demand can have a number of ramifications. At one extreme, most of the legislation may never come up for consideration. At the other extreme, most of the legislation may be passed through the system with very little quality control. At either extreme there are risks of external costs. The data for American state legislatures in 1981 suggest that both extremes do exist. For bills in the chamber of origin, the chamber passage rate ranges from less than 10 percent to more than 80 percent. Reformers seem to be primarily concerned, however, with quality control and the need for committee screening to hold down the flow of bills (e.g., Rosenthal, 1974). This should not cause us to lose sight of the fact that badly needed legislation can get buried, and often does, in the briefcases of committee chiefs.

How is it possible to have both quality control and the expeditious handling of legislation? The answer to this question may be better understood if we consider the decision-making environment of the typical legislator. Such a legislator will serve on a number of legislative committees and will be confronted by dozens of bills each week, many of which require that he further interact with colleagues in order to obtain their views and to bargain over the outcomes. Faced with excessive amounts of legislation, the legislator will be forced to simplify the way he or she makes decisions. For example, if there are too many bills, the legislator may not read those that appear to be less important, may not attempt to learn about the views of other legislators, or may abandon attempts to bargain. The adverse consequences become apparent if such conditions are extreme. Either most bills are dead at the outset, or most legislative measures are approved in a careless manner. The committee systems are designed to come to the rescue.

An open-input system with procedurally efficient methods of dealing seriously with legislation is likely to be judged more representative

---

1. A "closed-input" system would either place a specific limit on the number of proposals a member may introduce, or would specify who in the chamber is not eligible to sponsor proposals. From time to time some state legislatures have set such limits, but the practice is uncommon. Limits on amendments offer another way of reducing at least ad hoc proposals.

than a system attached merely to notions of full consensus. The external costs resulting from the lack of full participation or unanimity may be small compared to those resulting from inability to review a substantial agenda. When standing committees or subcommittees are given ample autonomy, more legislation can be given serious consideration.

Increasing Representation by Reducing Complexity

If the conditions under which decisions are made are too complex to allow legislators to evaluate information and estimate consequences, how can legislators cope with the problem? In a legislative body it is helpful to distinguish between two types of complexity. The first is introduced by the sheer volume of substantive material put forth as formal proposals. The second type is the result of the collective nature of choice in such an institution.

Volume of Legislation

The volume of material put forth as legislative proposals affects the amount of time and energy necessary to understand and process the material, and it has an impact on what may be called "decision costs." Decision costs are incurred by learning about the substance of legislative proposals and the affected environment, and by making up one's mind about their worth. But excessive volume can also create risk and, thereby, external costs. Greater risk is assumed whenever proposal content is ignored or considered carelessly.

What are the coping strategies for dealing with volume in a legislative organization? The most notable are:

1. *Devote attention to legislation involving substantial net benefits and/or whose outcome is in doubt.* The legislator makes guesses about which alternatives have the greatest $B - C$ values or whose probability of passage is near 0.5 (relative to other alternatives). One of several possible indexes, for example, would be $p(1 - p)(B - C)$, where $p =$ probability that the legislation will be approved, $B =$ benefits, and $C =$ costs. We need not wonder why the lion's share of legislative attention is given to a small number of controversial issues. While we would expect

legislators in any case to give more attention to such issues, a crowded agenda means that a greater proportion of proposals are never considered. The legislator may not have time to assess the benefits of most legislation, and thus whatever is at the front end of the agenda has the best chance of surviving. This coping strategy is not a solution to the problem but is really an elaboration of why the problem exists.

2. *Increase the length of the legislative session.* Many American states have moved in this direction, but Congress has almost reached its limit. Lengthening the legislative session creates opportunity costs for members with private occupations. A longer session also usually means that additional legislation will be introduced, perhaps at the same rate as in a shorter session.

3. *Increase staffing.* Staff members can aid in the search for and consolidation of policy-related information, or they can free legislators from other duties (e.g., constituency service) to allow legislators to devote more time to legislation. Both Congress and the state legislatures have greatly increased staff support over the last twenty years.

4. *Follow the lead of the chief executive.* Legislators may adopt a simple decision-making rule such as: "Vote the governor's position on a bill; if the governor has taken no position, vote against it." Such a rule could be expanded or altered to take into account chamber party leader positions. The rationale for adopting such a rule could be based on the confidence members have in the superior resources such leaders retain for evaluating legislation. The "followers" may also anticipate future side payments in return for their support.

5. *Use autonomous or semiautonomous standing committees and/ or subcommittees.* Most American legislatures employ semiautonomous committees—committees that can kill legislation (with exceptions), but that must send all approved measures to the next highest level for consideration. A legislator can ignore *non-personal* agenda items held back in those committees of which he is not a member. Such items may constitute two-thirds of the total agenda. For example, if a legislator serves on two of twenty committees in a one-hundred-member chamber, he may review only 10 percent of the legislation in committee. If the other committees report out only 25 percent of their proposals, the legislator needs to review or read only 32.5 percent of the proposals $(.25(.9) + .10)$, plus the few proposals he sponsored that did not make it out of other committees. Of course he may not need to review many proposals assigned to his own committees if subcommittees are employed.

All of the above strategies may have the effect of reducing the complexity of the decision-making environment. This does not mean that all such strategies are necessarily desirable. Legislators can make poor guesses about the value of legislation. They may find that longer legislative sessions create offsetting costs. Increased staffing sometimes creates more problems than it solves. To rely on the positions of the chief executive is to run the risk of alienating the home district. And the use of a committee-subcommittee system can make members vulnerable to the influence of pressure groups. Nevertheless, the problem does not go away by itself. Legislators need ways to simplify their options and to manage an agenda.

Collective Choice

The second source of complexity in legislatures is found in the use of majority voting to determine decision outcomes. This counting rule for tallying preferences is practiced normally on all occasions—floor decisions, standing committee decisions, and subcommittee decisions. In the U.S., only minor variations exist, for example, where a majority of those present is distinguished from an absolute majority, or where larger majorities are needed for certain types of action such as a veto override or constitutional amendment.

Majority voting, in conjunction with substantial quantities of legislation, introduces interpersonal complexities. Interpersonal complexities are of two kinds. The first is encountered in attempts to understand the preferences of other participants. The second is encountered in the process of bargaining and compromise. To understand the significance of these phenomena, it is necessary to refer to individual preference matrices. Making the normal assumption that individuals have transitive preference orderings, we may let $R(k, A)$ define an ordered matrix, where an individual has preferences of Pass or Defeat over M issues, $A(1), \ldots, A(M)$, and where there are 2^M possible outcomes, $k(1), \ldots, k(2^M)$. To illustrate we take four proposals and elaborate all possible preference patterns, each of which is a possible outcome:

Proposals According to Saliency

	1	2	3	4	
	P	P	P	P	Most preferred outcome
Case I	P	P	P	D	
	P	P	D	P	

	P	P	D	D
	P	D	P	P
	P	D	P	D
Preference Order of	P	D	D	P
Possible Outcomes,	P	D	D	D
	D	P	P	P
$2^M = 16$	D	P	P	D
	D	P	D	P
	D	P	D	D
	D	D	P	P
	D	D	P	D
	D	D	D	P
	D	D	D	D	Least preferred outcome

How complex is this preference matrix?[2]

At first glance it is tempting to define complexity by the size of the matrix, $M(2^M)$, which gives the number of cells in the matrix. The problem with this formulation, however, is that some 4 × 16 matrices are more complex than others. The above illustration, for example, can be produced uniquely by the person's preference for Pass or Defeat on each proposal, plus the fact that the member

1. prefers to win on proposal $A(1)$ more than winning on the other three proposals taken together;

2. prefers to win on proposal $A(2)$ more than winning on proposals $A(3)$ and $A(4)$ taken together;

3. prefers to win on proposal $A(3)$ more than winning on proposal $A(4)$.

In other words, seven preference relations, one for Pass or Defeat on each of the four proposals and one for each of the above three statements linking the saliency of the proposals, are enough to produce the complete matrix. The simplicity of the array is explained by the fact that the preferences are "separable." The outcome on one proposal has no effect upon the legislator's preferences on the other proposals. He prefers each

---

2. The assumption here of *strict preference orderings*, apparent in these illustrations, was adopted only after considering whether "indifferences" would substantially affect the analysis. There is first the question of whether a person is really very often indifferent between two alternatives when one of the alternatives must be selected, especially in a legislative setting. Second, the use of indifference relationships substantially complicates the model without altering the overall results. In other words, I have selected the simplest model that illustrates the basic features of complexity in a committee decision-making game. This does not preclude experimentation and refinement with weak preference orderings.

to pass regardless of the fate of the others, even though he prefers to win on some proposals more than others. In a situation of this kind, the legislator would have little difficulty in establishing his priorities. Furthermore, it would not be difficult for a colleague to understand the preferences of this legislator.

Another example of separable preferences occurs when a legislator prefers to win on all four issues, but short of that on any three issues, and short of that on any two issues, and so on. Again a unique configuration would be produced from a small number of preference statements. The preference setting can become much more complex, however, if the preferences are "inseparable," where the outcome preference on one proposal depends upon the outcome of another proposal. To illustrate this property of inseparability, a four-issue case will suffice:

	Proposals			
	1	*2*	*3*	*4*
	D	D	D	D
	P	P	P	P
Case II	D	P	P	P
	P	D	D	D
	D	D	D	P
	P	P	D	D
	P	P	P	D
Preference Order of	D	P	P	D
Possible Outcomes,	D	P	D	D
	D	D	P	P
$2^M = 16$	P	P	D	P
	P	D	P	P
	D	P	D	P
	P	D	P	D
	P	D	D	P
	D	D	P	D

In this case the legislator prefers most that all proposals are defeated (DDDD), but secondarily that all proposals pass (e.g., a subsidy for one group warrants a subsidy for three other groups, even though it would be better if none had a subsidy). Such contingencies make it *impossible to deduce the order of preferred outcomes from the saliency of the proposals*. While the above example was made fairly simple in order that it could be explained, inseparable preferences can describe patterns that appear to be nearly random. In such a situation, we have no basis for knowing the order of the outcome preference sets.

In order to understand the complexity of a situation involving the fate of several proposals, it is necessary to consider the structure of preferences. Legislators need to learn about each others' preference structures in order to bargain efficiently. In sum, there are at least three factors that affect the complexity of the game:

1. The number of proposals.[3]
2. The number of decision makers.
3. The structure of preferences.

Is there some way to minimize complexity? If so, legislators may be able to make decisions that will minimize decision costs per proposal and also the risks of external costs.

Minimum and Maximum Preference Complexity

One of the difficulties in evaluating decision-making complexity is that there is no known feasible way to measure or scale the structural complexity of preferences (as expressed in the preference matrix) in a practical setting. One alternative is to define the extremes mathematically. We can begin by defining *preference complexity* as

> the minimal number of preference inequalities necessary to produce complete information on outcome preferences over M issues.

For convenience of expression, we can let the sign ">" substitute for the phrase "is preferred to," and the use of which represents a preference inequality.

Minimum Preference Complexity is found when the preference structure is in its simplest form, when the complete matrix of outcome preferences can be produced from the fewest possible preference statements. For a single individual this quantity may be defined as

$$Cmin = 2M - 1 \qquad\qquad 9.1$$

where *Cmin* is the minimum number of preference inequalities necessary to produce the entire preference matrix, and M = the number of

---

3. It is clear that some proposals are more complex than others because they may include more sub-issues. Such a modification would need to be made in particular applications. The "budget bill" is a typical example.

proposals to be voted upon. For a proof that this is the minimum see Appendix I. For an entire group of legislators the minimum preference complexity is thus:

$$Cmin = N(2M - 1) \qquad 9.2$$

Maximum Preference Complexity, as indicated earlier, occurs when the preference outcomes are ordered randomly. In such a case, only the last preference outcome would be deducible, and thus the number of preference statements necessary can be enumerated as follows:

$$k(1) > k(2) > k(3) > \ldots > k(2^M)$$

Thus we may state that for a single individual:

$$Cmax = 2^M - 1 \qquad 9.3$$

and for a group the maximum is specified as

$$Cmax = N(2^M - 1) \qquad 9.4$$

The range of complexity between *Cmin* and *Cmax* will depend upon the values of *M* and *N*, the number of proposals and the number of decision makers. For example, Table 9.1 illustrates the calculations of *Cmin* and *Cmax* values for a variety of conditions. The degree of complexity can vary widely when three or more proposals are considered.

Table 9.1 Illustrative Cmin and Cmax Values for Increasing Numbers of Members and Proposals

		Number of Proposals (M)					
	N	*1*	*2*	*3*	*4*	*5*	*6*
Cmin	3	3	9	15	21	27	33
Cmax	3	3	9	21	45	93	189
Cmin	4	4	12	20	28	36	44
Cmax	4	4	12	28	60	124	252
Cmin	5	5	15	25	35	45	55
Cmax	5	5	15	35	75	155	315
Cmin	6	6	18	30	42	54	66
Cmax	6	6	18	42	90	186	378
Cmin	7	7	21	35	49	63	77
Cmax	7	7	21	49	105	217	441

Using the Committee System to Minimize Complexity

The above formulations offer a completely explicit way of representing preference complexity. It is apparent that such complexity may be reduced by assigning proposals to different and at least semiautonomous standing committees. In most situations each decision maker would encounter fewer participants and fewer proposals. In addition, it makes sense to assign unrelated proposals to different committees and any set of related proposals to the same committee. In this way the assignments will be more likely to coincide with separable subsets of inseparable preferences. Is there any way to know, however, just how many committees are desirable? In the long term such a question requires a great deal of empirical work, but headway can be made through the use of logical methods as well.

An Example. To illustrate we can let S = the number of committees, N = the number of members, and M = the number of proposals, and assume that:

1. Each committee is assigned the same number of members.
2. Each committee is assigned the same number of proposals.
3. Each member receives one committee assignment.
4. Each committee reports out exactly one bill for floor vote.

We might label this example the "equal work-single assignment" case. Clearly, I have made the above assumptions to produce a nontedious result. More general equations than those below are in Appendix 9.2 of this chapter. Overall conclusions derived here would not be affected by specifying the assumptions differently.

From equations 9.2 and 9.4, the preference complexity of *floor* consideration has a minimum and maximum of:

$$Cmin = N(2S - 1) \qquad Cmax = N(2^S - 1)$$

where Assumption #4 allows the substitution of S for M.

Since each standing committee has the same number of members, N/S, and the same number of proposals, M/S, the total preference complexity for all committees at minimum and maximum levels may be written as follows (substituting in equations 9.2 and 9.4):

$$Cmin = S(N/S)(2M/S - 1) \qquad Cmax = S(N/S)((2^{M/S}) - 1)$$
$$= N(2M/S - 1) \qquad = N((2^{M/S}) - 1)$$

The above alternatives make it possible to consider combinations of committee and floor conditions, minimum complexity on the floor and in committees, maximum complexity in both, and minimum complexity in one and maximum in the other.

From the above equations we are able to utilize standard minimizing procedures to solve for complexity. In the first case, it is assumed that minimum complexity conditions apply to both floor and committee proceedings, where

$$Cmin = N(2S - 1) + N(2M/S - 1)$$

and minimizing $Cmin$ with respect to S (minimizing complexity with respect to the number of committees) we take the partial derivative, where $dCmin/dS = 0$ and

$$N(2 - 2M/S^2) = 0$$
$$N2 - N2M/S^2 = 0$$
$$N2 = N2M/S^2$$
$$1 = M/S^2$$
$$S^2 = M$$
$$S = \sqrt{M} \text{ where the second derivative,}$$
$$d^2Cmin/dS^2 = N(4MS/S^4)$$

Applying the same procedures when maximum complexity exists on both the floor and in committees, we obtain:

$$Cmax = N(2^S - 1) + N(2^{M/S} - 1)$$
$$N(2^S + 2^{M/S} - 2)$$
$$dCmax/dS = N(2^S(\ln 2) + 2^{M/S}(\ln 2)(-M/S^2)) = 0$$
$$2^S(\ln 2) = (2^{M/S}(\ln 2)M)/S^2$$
$$2^S = (2^{M/S}(M))/S^2$$
$$(S^2)2^S = M2^{M/S} \quad \text{(Note that for } S^2 \text{ to equal}$$
$$S^2 = M \qquad\qquad M, \ 2^S \text{ must equal } 2^{M/S})$$
$$S = \sqrt{M}$$

9.5

The result is the same as for $Cmin$. Complexity is at a minimum when the number of committees equals the square root of the number of proposals. Conversely, if the number of committees is a given, preference complexity conditions are minimized if the expected number of proposals is that number squared.

A special result like the above is a function of the assumptions, thus we might expect a different solution when minimum complexity conditions exist on the floor but maximum complexity conditions exist in committees. Referring to these mixed conditions as *Cmix* and using the same procedure, we obtain:

$$Cmix = N(2S - 1) + N(2^{M/S} - 1)$$
$$N(2S + 2^{M/S} - 2)$$
$$dCmix/dS = N[2 + (2^{M/S}(\ln 2))(-M/S^2)] = 0$$

which reduces to

$$2S^2 = .69M2^{M/S}$$
$$S = (.347M2^{M/S})^{1/2}$$

9.6

To illustrate the results in Equations 9.5 and 9.6, we can take as a given the number of committees established by a legislative chamber, and then ask for the number of proposals the system is designed to process in a single "production cycle." That is, assuming that preference complexity is to be minimized, and excluding at this point the use of subcommittees, what advice can be obtained? Taking three examples:

# of Committees	Eq 9.5	Eq 9.6
$S = 10$	$M = 100$	$M = 32$
$S = 20$	$M = 400$	$M = 78$
$S = 30$	$M = 900$	$M = 130$

As may be observed, when preference complexity structure is the same at the chamber and committee levels, the number of committees relative to the number of proposals is small. But if it is assumed that proposals reaching the floor stimulate separable preferences, while those in each committee stimulate inseparable and highly complex preferences, then a relatively large number of committees is desirable. The average number of proposals per committee under Equation 9.6 ranges only from 3.2 to 4.3, or approximately 3 to 5 proposals per committee.

To take another example, suppose that a production cycle were defined by a "call of the roll," where each member is allowed to introduce one proposal. In a fifty-member group, homogeneous separability conditions would suggest that seven committees would be optimum, whereas for *Cmix*, fourteen committees would be optimum. These numbers do reflect the very strict constraints set forth earlier. What is important to note, however, is that an *organizational decision to separate proposals into separable subsets of inseparable issues, if in fact this can be done, makes a major difference in what is structurally optimal.*

To fully illustrate preference complexity under varying conditions, we can utilize the above minimizing solutions to estimate *preference complexity values*, first assuming there were no committees, and then assuming chamber review of only committee approved legislation. To illustrate:

$$\text{Let } M = 50, N = 50$$

FULL CHAMBER CONSIDERATION ONLY

A. Separable Preferences (Using *Cmin*)
$N(2M - 1) = 50(2(50) - 1) = 4950$

B. Inseparable Preferences (Using *Cmax*)
$N(2^M - 1) = 50(2^{50} - 1)$
$\qquad\qquad = 5.6295 \quad 16 \quad$ (scientific notation)

COMMITTEE CONSIDERATION AND CHAMBER REVIEW OF APPROVED BILLS

C. Separable Preferences at Both Levels (Using *Cmin*)
$N(2S - 1) + N(2M/S - 1) = 50(2(7) - 1) + 50(2(50/7) - 1)$
$\qquad\qquad\qquad\qquad\qquad = 1314$

D. Inseparable Preferences at Both Levels (Using *Cmax*)
$N(2^S - 1) + N(2^{M/S} - 1) = 50(2^7 - 1) + 50(2^{7.14} - 1) = 13,366$

E. Separable on Floor, Inseparable in Committee (Using *Cmix*)
$N(2S - 1) + N(2^{M/S} - 1) = 50(2(14) - 1) + 50(2^{3.57} - 1) = 1,894$

These abstract solutions illustrate that the impact of committee use is especially dramatic when preferences are inseparable, and when such conditions can be delegated to committees rather than confronted on the floor of the chamber (as in case E).

The above example demonstrates in a precise way the major reductions in complexity that can be achieved by paying attention to the distinction between separable and inseparable preferences. A fair question here is whether legislators have any knowledge of such distinctions until after the fact. That is, can legislative leaders foretell which kinds of proposals are likely to be highly related to each other (thus stimulating inseparable preferences), and thereby construct committee subject-matter areas and assign proposals accordingly? It seems to me that this is exactly what legislators do, but with varying skill and foresight. In fact, we might argue that when related proposals are assigned to different committees very often, it is a signal that reorganization may be desirable in order to bring such proposals to a common forum within a single committee.

Subcommittees

For the American states most observers would probably agree that due to the increased volume of legislation, the use of subcommittees has increased substantially over the last twenty years. In most states, however, their use remains much less formal than in the U.S. Congress. Almost one-third of survey respondents indicated that the use of subcommittees was not very common in their experience, and only 17 percent indicated that subcommittees were required by their chamber rules. Most illustrative of the status of subcommittee use were the responses to the following inquiry:

Some state legislatures now use subcommittees frequently. What is the status of this practice in your chamber? (Please check)

Subcommittees are an official part of my chamber rules and at least some committees are required to use them.	344
Subcommittees are used on a regular basis in many committees, but it is really up to the chairman of the committee to decide in each session whether they will be used.	1028
Subcommittees are not very common but they tend to be used in an informal manner in some committees.	543
To my knowledge subcommittees have not been used.	95
	$N = 2010$

Subcommittees are used more frequently in the larger lower chambers. For example, in only ten of forty-nine lower chambers did respondents indicate that subcommittees were not very common or not used. In the senate chambers, nearly half (23) were described as having little subcommittee use. In sum, the responses suggest that about one-third of the chambers exhibit low subcommittee use. Two states had unusual practices. In Iowa a subcommittee was appointed for each bill that was assigned to a committee. As a consequence, each member served on a very large number of subcommittees. In the Utah legislature, the members all serve on appropriations "subcommittees," but since the full committee includes the entire membership, the subcommittees are really in fact no different from committees.

Legislators were asked two other questions about subcommittees. They were asked to specify on how many they served and to indicate whether "important committees relied upon subcommittee reports." The correlations between "subcommittee use," reliance upon subcommittee reports, and the mean number of subcommittee assignments range between 0.59 and 0.65 ($n = 99$), suggesting that the questions tap into different aspects of the same phenomenon.

Scholars have long noted, especially with regard to Congress, that larger chambers have been more formal and rigid in their rules. Since there are more members to introduce bills and amendments and since the bargaining complexity is geometrically increased, the members in larger chambers are frequently forced to set more severe limits on debate and floor action. The creation of a committee system also takes on greater dimensions in large chambers. In Figure 9.1, we can see that members or leaders in larger chambers appoint more committees ($r = .37$ and larger committees ($r = .65$). Larger committees are more likely to utilize subcommittees ($r = .43$) and to utilize subcommittee reports ($r = .44$).

The point to be taken from the analysis is that subcommittees follow naturally in an attempt to process the agenda efficiently. Just as a large chamber needs committees, a large committee needs subcommittees. In large chambers the leaders have more members to place on committees and thus must decide whether to accommodate them through size or number. To the extent that they choose the former, subcommittees will follow. Whether any particular committee actually uses subcommittees will depend in part on how many proposals it receives. The decisions about how many committees to have and of what size can have a major impact on the ability of members to cope with the demands made on them.

An effective committee system makes it unnecessary for a legislator to learn about proposals and consequences if the proposals are not on his personal agenda and if the proposals die in committees of which he is not a member. Subcommittees, if they are given similar powers, economize in the same manner. The use of standing committees and subcommittees makes it less complex to bargain and easier to learn about the preferences of other voting members.

Traces of these effects are not so easy to discover, since every chamber employs committees and the amount of legislation they receive varies widely. Nevertheless, we are able to examine the reported time legislators spend in various types of committee activity, allowing "time" to serve as our proxy for costs. Table 9.2 illustrates that the time-costs of seeking information about the positions of other members (taken as a percentage of total time-costs) increases with committee size ($r = .22$), even though, as shown earlier, increased committee size often leads to increased subcommittee use. Where subcommittee use is a conse-

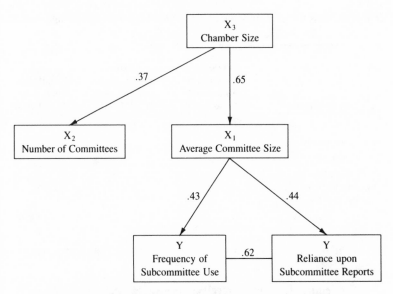

Spurious Relationships: $r_{x_1 x_2} = .20$; $r_{y_1 x_3} = .28$; $r_{y_2 y_3} = .30$

Fig. 9.1 Relationship between Chamber Size and Four Committee
System Characteristics

quence, as demonstrated by the three separate measures in Table 9.2, legislators appear to shift their activities somewhat, from acquiring information about proposals to bargaining over them. We might speculate that the use of subcommittees in and of itself probably means a busy agenda—that is, there are too many proposals or the subject matter is too complex for the committee as a whole to handle. Subcommittees not only reduce the number of proposals each member must consider, but they allow each member the opportunity to bargain with some realistic chance of locating equilibrium choices (e.g., see Shepsle, 1979).

How does the above discussion fit into the previous mathematical analysis of complexity reduction? First, it does appear that the use of subcommittees brings into play the kind of interpersonal behavior that we expect when inseparable issues need to be resolved. Second, it can be seen, theoretically, that subcommittees are to a standing committee what standing committees are to the entire legislature. Presumably, proposals that stimulate inseparable preferences should be assigned to a subcommittee—separable from other subsets of inseparable preferences, since those proposals respectively are assigned to other subcommittees. In an extraordinarily efficient system the proposals are parceled

Table 9.2   Relationship between Committee Characteristics and Time-Costs (correlation matrix, N = 99)

Characteristic	Proposal Information Time-Costs (% of Total)	Member Information Time-Costs (% of Total)	Bargaining Time-Costs (% of Total)
Average Committee Size		.22	
Subcommittee Use	−.19		.25
Number of Subcommittee Assignments	−.29		.31
Subcommittee Reports in Important Committees	−.29		.25

Only r values where p < .05 are reported in order to illustrate a pattern. These correlations do not take into account variance within chambers, which cannot be separated from reporting error.

out such that (See Appendix 9.2 of this chapter for representative equation):

1. The entire legislature receives proposals that elicit separable preferences.
2. The committee receives proposals that elicit separable preferences.
3. The subcommittee receives proposals that elicit inseparable preferences.

It is certainly true that no known legislature is so efficient, and no less true that legislators in any setting can complicate matters by offering amendments or by engaging in logrolling. These truths in no way contradict the argument. Instead they ask for additional analyses that go beyond the scope of this project. We can simply point out here that to minimize complexity, the above conditions may be necessary if not sufficient.[4]

Conclusion

Concern for representation in American legislatures arises when legislative decisions are delegated to standing committees and their subcom-

---

4. In preliminary formal analysis of complexity minimization, for example, it has been found that a committee-subcommittee system does not necessarily outperform a simple standing committee system. The central determinant is the number of legislative proposals.

mittees. Such delegations mean that fewer elected legislators are likely to have a vote on the outcome of many if not most proposals. The argument is made here that a more serious problem can result from the inability of the legislature to offer serious deliberation over an ample proportion of legislative proposals. The standing committee and subcommittee system allows a division of labor that enhances the processing of the agenda.

In constructing a standing committee-subcommittee system, procedural efficiency is important to the extent that a larger proportion of legislative measures receive formal consideration and resolution. Central to the efficiency of the system is the degree to which the organizational structure accommodates the structure of human preferences. The complexity of the decision-making environment is a significant determinant of the quality of legislative deliberation. The crowded agendas of legislatures make it necessary to seek ways to reduce the complexity of decision making. This is accomplished by applying fewer members to fewer issues, and by taking into account the distinction between separable and inseparable preferences. The restricted complexity minimization model, in its alternative forms, illustrates that it is possible to estimate optimal organizational structures by taking into account the complexity of human preferences.

Relatively little is known about the use of subcommittees in the fifty U.S. state legislatures. Subcommittees have not been standardized or well documented in official records. Evidence in this study does suggest, however, that their use has had an impact upon allocations of time to bargaining and negotiation. In other words, such activities can be conducted most profitably in settings not disadvantaged by overwhelming complexity. Subcommittees are more likely to offer situations wherein inseparable preferences can be negotiated and resolved.

Appendix 9.1

For an informal proof to show that $2M - 1$ is the minimum number of preference inequalities necessary to produce the entire preference matrix, the following steps may be taken:

1. When the preferences on proposals are separable, a member prefers passage $(P > D)$ or defeat $(D > P)$ on each proposal regardless of the outcome of other proposals, such that

$$A(1), \qquad A(2), \qquad \ldots, \qquad A(M)$$
$$P \text{ or } D, \qquad P \text{ or } D, \qquad \ldots, \qquad P \text{ or } D$$

Thus the number of Pass/Defeat preferences equals M.

2. Assuming strict transitivity, a member ranks the proposals according to their saliency, such that

$$A(1) > A(2) > A(3) > \ldots > A(M)$$

Thus there are $M - 1$ necessary preference statements related to saliency.

3. The same number of preference statements are needed to produce

$$A(1) > [A(2) \text{ and } A(3) \ldots \text{ and } A(M)], A(2) > [A(2) \ldots$$
$$\text{and } A(M)], A(3) > \ldots > A(M).$$

which may be reduced to

$$A(1) > [A(2) > [A(3) > \ldots > A(M)] \ldots]$$

For example, the above formulation solves for the preference matrix in CASE I illustrated earlier. For notational convenience, let the proposals be designated as A, B, C, and D, where

$$A > B > C > D$$
$$\text{and} \qquad A > (B > (C > D))$$

4. When the number of preference statements due to saliency is added to the number of Pass/Defeat preferences, the preference complexity for one member is

$$M + (M - 1) = 2M - 1$$

5. When there are N members, each having separable preferences of minimum complexity,

$$Cmin = N(2M - 1)$$

Appendix 9.2

The assumptions made for the example in the text allow the efficient calculation of partial derivatives according to standard minimization procedures. That is, it was possible to minimize "preference complexity," as explicitly defined, with respect to particular variables such as the number of committees. If these simplifying assumptions are not made for the purpose of examining the relationship between the number of committees and the number of bills when complexity is minimized, it will be necessary to work with the calculation formulas presented below.

I. FULL MEMBERSHIP CONSIDERATION ONLY

Separable Preferences $\qquad N(2M - 1)$

Inseparable Preferences $\qquad N(2^M - 1)$

II. ASSIGNMENT TO COMMITTEES, FULL MEMBERSHIP REVIEW OF COMMITTEE APPROVED BILLS ONLY

Separable Preferences $\qquad N(2P - 1)$

$$+ \sum_1^s n_i (2m_i - 1)$$

Inseparable Preferences in Committee Only $\qquad N(2^P - 1)$

$$+ \sum_1^s n_i (2^{m_i} - 1)$$

III. ASSIGNMENT TO SUBCOMMITTEES, COMMITTEE REVIEW OF SUBCOMMITTEE APPROVED BILLS ONLY, FULL MEMBERSHIP REVIEW OF COMMITTEE APPROVED BILLS ONLY

Separable Preferences $\qquad N(2P - 1)$

$$+ \sum_1^s n_i (2p_i - 1)$$

$$+ \sum_1^s \sum_1^b n_i'(2m_i' - 1)$$

Inseparable Preferences in Subcommittee Only $\qquad N(2^P - 1)$

$$+ \sum_{1}^{s} n_i \, (2p_i - 1)$$

$$+ \sum_{1}^{s} \sum_{1}^{b} n_i' (2^{m_i'} - 1)$$

KEY: N = Number of Members, M = Number of Proposals

        P = Number of Proposals reported out of Committees

        n_i = Number of members in Committee i

        m_i = Number of proposals in Committee i

        p_i = Number of proposals reported out of subcommittees in a committee i

        n_i' = Number of members in Subcommittee i

        m_i' = Number of proposals in Subcommittee i

        s = Number of committees in Chamber

        b = Number of subcommittees in Committee i

10

The Complex Committee Game

Within the context of constitutional sanctions in the United States, the standing committees of the various legislatures have evolved along similar patterns. As the volume of demand for action in the form of legislative proposals has increased, responsibility for processing legislation has devolved upon the committees and their subcommittees. The elected party leaders and the chief executive no doubt have a major influence over what items are placed at the top of the agenda, but, with rare exception, such items must undergo the scrutiny of the committees. To counterbalance the weight of the leadership, committee chairs and rank-and-file legislators have agendas of their own. In addition, the sources of demand for change are widespread, found among countless national, state, and local interest group leaders as well as among the legislators themselves.

Evidence amassed for both Congress (Westefield, 1974; Shepsle, 1978; Ray and Smith, 1984) and the states would suggest that, typically, in order to meet in part this extraordinary demand, the legislative leadership begins the legislative session by practicing accommodation in making committee assignments, including enlarging committees for which there is a surplus of requests for membership. Committee chairmanships are also a potential source of contention. Such positions are in scarce supply in Congress, but the problem is solved there by having a multitude of subcommittee chairmanships. In the states, where seniority is much less a factor, legislative leaders are more likely to use political preferences and leverage in making chair appointments. State legislative party leaders frequently have more freedom, however, to create new committees to accommodate members' ambitions.

The historical pattern over thirty years (1950–1984) has shown a decline in the number of committees in almost all legislative chambers in the states. The trend lines vary considerably, usually illustrating several increases and decreases in the number of committees, and sometimes characterized by a single major reduction. Reorganizations into fewer but larger committees in state legislative chambers has no doubt helped spawn the use of subcommittees. And likewise, the prospect of subcommittee use may offer sufficient reason to reduce the number of standing committees.

Why are legislative leaders so accommodating in the committee assignment process? A common observation is that they are simply in a weak position, for example, relative to the party leaders in parliamentary bodies. The reelection of a legislator in the U.S. depends much less on support of the party leadership than in most countries with parliamentary systems. A second reason, of equal or greater significance, is that legislators are not playing a zero-sum game. The leaders, for example, can have their way on a number of important legislative matters, yet not find it necessary to prevent other members from deriving benefits also. Such cooperation can be encouraged by doling out as many favors as possible in the committee assignment process.

Leadership accommodation solutions to these committee preference "puzzles" do not necessarily bring about solutions to policy preference puzzles; however, distributive policies, as defined in Lowi (1964), allow members to "pork barrel" for their districts in omnibus legislation (Ferejohn, 1974). Leaders and followers alike incorporate their district projects into major budget or appropriation approvals. Such projects are believed to bring in support in future elections. In this regard, several scholars have noted the norm of "universalism" (Polsby, 1968; Mayhew, 1974; Weingast, 1979) with respect to Congress. Universalism refers in this context to the unopposed inclusion of legislators' projects in an omnibus bill produced by a committee. Weingast is able to show logically why such an approach (called the Universal Legislative Game) makes sense, for example, when compared to situations in which minimal winning coalitions are sought (called the Distributive Legislative Game).

Most governors in the U.S. have the item veto. This is an extraordinary tool in the hands of a single actor and can severely restrict a legislator's success in obtaining projects for the district. An uncooperative governor may be able to wreck the "universal legislative game" by selectively vetoing the projects of legislators. The President of the United States does not have the item veto and will have great difficulty undoing an omnibus package. President Carter learned this lesson the hard way at the beginning of his term when he opposed public works legislation to build dams. Many of the projects were at best marginal on a benefit-cost basis. Carter had to veto either everyone's dam or no dam at all.

So how can most state legislators respond to their dilemma? Not only are governors blessed with the item veto, but also the states have severe budget-balancing restrictions. Deficit financing is not open-ended. Estimated revenues act as a cap on appropriations, and in many states the governor has the power to withhold funds from expenditure categories if the legislature was too optimistic. The legislators have no choice but to "take it one step at a time."

To the individual legislator with an agenda, the *first* major hurdle is the standing committee or its subcommittee. The legislator increases the chances of bill sponsorship success if:

1. He or she is a member of the committees (or subcommittees) to which personal agenda items are assigned, and
2. personal agenda items in fact do come up for committee-subcommittee consideration.

Organizational efficiency is an important matter, especially to those members without the access or influence to have their items positioned early in the committee agendas.

The *second* major hurdle occurs on the floor of the chamber (or possibly in the party caucus). If there is "reciprocity" among committees, action on the floor (or in caucus) is less likely to be conflictual and may appear to be little more than a routine processing of committee decisions. Floor or caucus decision making is further simplified if issues involving inseparable preferences have been taken up and settled at the standing committee or subcommittee level. Legislation surviving the standing committees and floor action may be subjected to conference committee action and gubernatorial action as well. Table 4.1 illustrates that the second chamber usually approves bills, with or without amendment, sent over by the first chamber (Median > 70%).

In sum, to maximize benefits, it is in the individual interest of most legislators to maximize chances for approval of their personal agendas. The greater the success in standing committees and the chamber of origin, the greater the success in the enactment of legislation (chapter 2). It is in the interest of legislators to act out a game scenario that produces high success at early stages in the process.

Scenario for Success

An important part of the game is spawned by leadership *accommodation in committee assignments*. As depicted in Figure 10.1, accommodation allows members to sort themselves out according to "saliency of preference." In other words, members will ask to serve on committees dealing with issues most important to them, the same committees

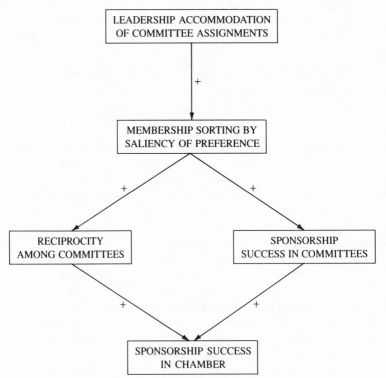

Fig. 10.1   Scenario for Sponsorship Success

through which they are likely to sponsor legislation. Because they serve on the committee they will have greater success in gaining committee approval. Committee approval makes it more likely that legislators will want reciprocity among committees, especially if they are on the committees dealing with issues most important to them. Reciprocity and committee approval will increase sponsorship success at the chamber level.

This scenario for sponsorship success may be seen as a conditional behavioral solution to the legislative policy making game. The same fundamental process could apply to a committee and its subcommittees (In Figure 10.1 simply insert "subcommittee" for committee and "committee" for chamber). A number of other factors, however, can decrease the effectiveness with which the game can be played.

Counterbalancing Inefficiencies

Committee assignment accommodation also leads to differentiation in committee size. To the extent that this leads to enlarging the more popular committees without reducing the size of other committees, legislators will receive an increased number of committee assignments. At the same time, when the leadership wishes to accommodate requests for committee chairmanships, one way to do it is to increase the number of committees. Again, such a change will tend to lead to an increased number of committee assignments.

An increase in the number of committee assignments may have little impact if the committees do not meet or consider legislation, but in the national survey of state legislators, complaint levels (by chamber) regarding "too many committee assignments" do correlate with the mean number of committee assignments ($r = .60$, $N = 99$). In order to illustrate this relationship, a scatterplot was examined and it was determined that a 20 percent complaint level in a chamber seemed to be a threshold. Using this criterion, data in Table 10.1 reveal that there is little difference in the complaint rate when three or fewer committee assignments per person are made. The proportion of chambers reaching the 20 percent complaint threshold, however, accelerates as the number of committee assignments increases.

Further examination of legislator responses reveals in fact that there are three different kinds of complaints that covary across the ninety-nine state legislative chambers:

1. Too many committee assignments (ASSIGN)
2. Scheduling and attendance problems (SCHED)
3. Committees dominated by the chairs (CHAIRDOM)

where (*r* values):

While data conditions do not warrant a formal path analysis of the above relationships, the results suggest that the number of committee assignments may be a key underlying factor in producing lower passage rates—mainly because too many assignments lead to scheduling problems and chair domination of committees. Leadership accommodation of preferences produces also a *counter-scenario*, as illustrated in Figure 10.2. Too much accommodation can lead to too many committee assignments, which then in turn can lead to scheduling problems and chair domination of committees. These latter two factors appear to have an adverse effect upon the bill passage rate, as shown in chapter 4 (Table 4.5).

Equilibrium

The above analysis implies that accommodation of committee assignment and chairmanship preferences can be carried too far. Increased accommodation will increase sponsorship success unless it leads also to

Table 10.1   Relationship between Mean Number of Committee Assignments and "Too Many Committee Assignments" Complaint

	Mean Number of Committee Assignments				
	2 or less	*2+ to 3*	*3+ to 4*	*4+ to 5*	*5+ or more*
Above 20% Complain	2 (10%)	4 (12%)	8 (31%)	7 (54%)	6 (100%)
20% or Less Complain	19 (90%)	29 (88%)	18 (69%)	6 (46%)	0
	21	33	26	13	6

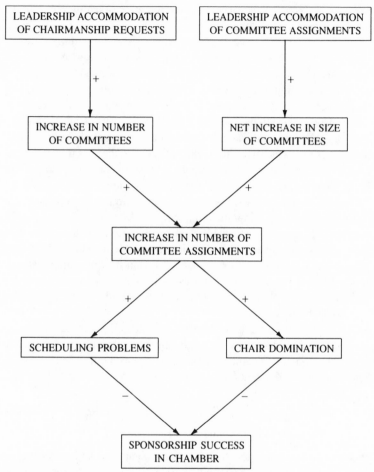

Fig. 10.2 Counter-Scenario to Sponsorship Success

too many committee assignments. *The search for the optimal set of accommodation moves can be seen as an equilibrium process.* The system reaches marginal equilibrium when any change in accommodation (more or less) leads to a decrease in sponsorship success. A number of factors affect the equilibrium, including the amount of legislation offered (which has increased dramatically in the last thirty years), the influx of new members every two years, and changes in preferences of returning members.

Changes in the environment and the distribution of legislation to

various subject areas also encourages the creation of additional committees or changes in the committee structure. For example, from the early
1960s to the 1970s a large number of states created committees on energy and environment. These new committees may or may not subsume
the subjects of older committees. In the 1980 Texas house, for instance,
there were committees on energy resources, environmental affairs, and
natural resources as well as committees on agriculture and livestock,
and transportation. In the California senate there were standing committees on agriculture and water resources, energy and public utilities, and
natural resources and wildlife, while in the house there were committees
on resource, land use and energy with a standing subcommittee on energy, a committee on transportation with a standing subcommittee on
air quality, a standing ways and means subcommittee on resources and
transportation, and a committee on water, parks and wildlife.

In spite of apparent difficulties in sorting out the issues, especially
in new areas of concentration, legislators are able to find ways of delegating issue responsibility to reduce decision-making complexity. A
more detailed examination of bill assignments, as was undertaken for
Indiana (chapter 2), will show normally that highly related legislation
will go to the same committee.

It is clear from the above analysis that the chamber leadership approach to committee and chair appointments is the key to the way in
which the committee game of legislating is played out. The leadership,
intentionally or unintentionally, can "over-accommodate." From the
equation:

$$\text{\# of Committee} = (\text{\# of Committees})(\text{Mean Size of}$$
$$\text{Assignments} \qquad \text{Committees})$$

the impact of accommodation is clear. Intentional and excessive increases in the number of committee assignments could be seen as playing into the hands of the committee chairs and chamber leadership.
Thus the equilibrium state described above may not be appealing to particular leadership coalitions.

Externalities

The incentive for efficient processing of legislation is strengthened by
the external or "whole life" circumstances that most legislators face. In
earlier chapters (5 and 6) we saw how opportunity costs can influence

legislator preferences for shorter legislative sessions. Legislators with substantial opportunity costs, owing to private occupation or family needs, are likely to see diminishing marginal returns with each additional day of legislative work required. Legislators who are "professionals," however, prefer to be full-time legislators and may very well support longer sessions for additional pay at the same rate. While these concerns are important, they are intermediate to long-term in nature. In the short-term (i.e., one legislative session or term), the self-interests of legislators may not be so disparate. Salaries for the session normally are fixed or limited and very few legislators are likely to benefit by per diem allowances over and above the minimum amount of time it takes to process the agenda. Thus as a whole, legislators are likely to benefit more in the short run by a system that processes legislation quickly and without the call for special sessions and overtime.

To the legislator the value of the legislative game is a function of the costs of playing the game and the net benefits derived from it. As we saw in chapter 5, the number of workdays required in the capital, and the success rate on legislation, are significant indicators of these costs and benefits, respectively. It is in the achievement of benefits that legislators have developed a number of interesting ways to proceed. The previous chapters have given evidence of both formal and informal adaptation in the behavior patterns of legislators.

Taking a longer view of state legislative histories, it would appear that five basic trends have occurred over approximately the last thirty years:

1. An increase in the amount of legislation.
2. An increase in the length or frequency of legislative sessions.
3. An increase in the amount of staffing.
4. A decrease in the number of standing committees.
5. An increase in the use of subcommittees.

These trends characterize an overwhelming proportion of states. At least three plausible explanations for these changes (mainly trends 2–5) can be put forward:

1. The need to exercise control over the executive.
2. An emulation of Congress and its attributes.
3. The need to process increasing amounts of legislation.

It seems reasonable to speculate that many of these changes have come about in response to growth in the executive and the need to coordinate legislative policy and control with executive activities. As the executive expands, it devotes increasing human resources to the formulation of policies requiring legislative approval. If the legislature is to legislate it must maintain control by devoting increasing amounts of time to the job, by hiring staff specialists, and by coordinating its organizational structure with the executive department's organization. No doubt many state legislatures received impetus from the reform movement of the 1960s, highlighted by the efforts of the Citizens Conference on State Legislatures in *The Sometimes Governments* (1971). It so happens that a great many of the suggestions of the Conference are taken directly from Congressional practices. And one cannot help noticing the similarity of these trends to the evolution of Congress.

Even though it is possible to attribute the legislative changes to inducements relating to legislative control of the executive, and to the cloning of Congressional procedure, it is nevertheless the case that the above trends are all consistent with the need to increase the ability of the legislative chamber to process greater amounts of legislation. Thus one may argue that individual legislator demands are a strong contributing factor to the internal dynamics that result in the above trends.

Appendix:
Survey Information

Several surveys were administered to obtain the information necessary for this work. All of the surveys were based upon the 1981 sessions. A copy of the main survey, the four page questionnaire sent to legislators in every state chamber, is included at the end of this appendix.

The Fifty-State Legislator Survey

The responses represent a return of 43 percent. Questionnaires were sent to sixty-six members of every house and thirty-three members of every senate (except when fewer members served in such chambers). Within each chamber the members were randomly selected. The original mailouts were made upon the close of legislative sessions, which meant that they were staggered according to length of session. Nonrespondents were sent two followup questionnaires. The primary purpose of the study was to conduct an analysis at the chamber level, and to that end our minimum number of responses for any chamber is seven. The mean exceeds twenty-one. The respondents make up 27 percent of all state legislators.

In total figures, house respondents represent 69 percent of the returns, compared to 74 percent of all legislators (Nebraska excluded). The Democrat-Republican ratio among respondents is 53–47. Majority party respondents make up about 25 percent of all majority party members.

The Legislative Workday and Bill Passage Surveys

Two non-opinion surveys were necessary to obtain vital information about each legislative chamber. In the first case, legislative service personnel were sent a questionnaire containing a monthly breakdown asking them to indicate the days of each week the legislators actually met within each month. While human error cannot be avoided entirely, the responses were detailed and of high quality, indicating the respondent had consulted official records. An expensive alternative method would require consulting each legislative journal and counting the days of official business recorded.

The second survey required determining the number of bills introduced and passed in the first and second chambers of each legislature. In many states we were sent official documents from which the information could be extracted (with varying degrees of difficulty). In other states, qualified personnel filled out a form we had sent along with the request. Our sources were often state librarians or the immediate professional service staff of the legislature. Completion of this survey required much telephoning and follow-up.

The Committee Membership Survey

This survey was the easiest to administer, since we were asking for nothing more than the committee membership roster for the year in question. We received complete committee lists for all chambers and were able to use these lists to verify questionnaire data as well as to determine committee size and the number of committees employed. For most states these lists do not include subcommittee assignments.

The Indiana–Missouri Surveys

For the 1981 sessions of the Indiana and Missouri legislatures, the official journal indexes were utilized to obtain individual bill sponsorship and success data. Members who retired voluntarily from the legislature after the 1981–82 term were sent a questionnaire to elicit their reasons for doing so. Of the sixty-three who voluntarily retired, forty-three responded satisfactorily. In Indiana 36 percent of the retirees were minority party members, compared to 34 percent for the entire legislature. In Missouri 42 percent were minority party retirees, compared to 32 percent minority party membership in the full body. There was no substantial evidence that minority party members have a greater tendency to retire.

State Legislative Survey

1. How many years have you served in the legislature? _____   Present chamber? _____
                                                                              House or Senate

   Party affiliation? _____   Date of birth (year)? _____

   Please indicate if during the most recent session you held any of the following positions:

   ( ) Committee Chair or Ranking Member of Committee
   ( ) Speaker, Majority or Minority Leader, or party whip
   ( ) Member of Policy Committee (skip if this is not a leadership committee)
   ( ) Subcommittee Chair   ( ) Other _____

   Have you held any of the above positions in prior sessions? ( ) yes   ( ) no

2. In your legislature, where would you say the most significant decisions are made? Please use numbers 1, 2, and 3 to order your top three choices, where "1" is your first choice.

   ( ) Party Caucus   ( ) Regular Committee Meetings   ( ) In Governor's Office

   ( ) In Policy Committee   ( ) Prelegislative Session   ( ) In Subcommittees

   ( ) On the Floor   ( ) Office of Presiding Offi-   ( ) Other _____
                                     cers or Majority Leaders   _____

3. From your experience in committee work, what would you regard as the ideal committee size (# of members) for the following types of committees?

   _____ a typical standing committee of your chamber,

   _____ a typical subcommittee (if appropriate to your chamber)

   Which of the following rules best describes the committee voting procedures in your chamber?

   ( ) In order to report a bill out favorably, voting support of only a majority of those present must be obtained (if quorum exists).

   ( ) In order to report a bill out favorably, voting support of a majority of the full committee membership must be obtained.

   If you have a committee quorum rule, what is it? _____

4. Some state legislatures now use subcommittees frequently. What is the status of this practice in your chamber? (please check)

   ( ) Subcommittees are an official part of my chamber rules and at least some committees are required to use them.

   ( ) Subcommittees are used on a regular basis in may committees, but it is really up to the chairman of the committee to decide in each session whether they will be used.

   ( ) Subcommittees are not very common but they tend to be used in an informal manner in some committees.

   ( ) To my knowledge subcommittees have not been used.

5. Where would you say partisanship is most evident in your chamber? (please check one)

   ( ) During floor proceedings   ( ) During committee proceedings

   ( ) During subcommittee proceedings   ( ) Not evident in my chamber

6. During the most recent session, how many regular committee assignments did you receive? ____
    How many of these committees actually handled legislation? _____
    How many <u>sub</u>committee assignments did you receive? _____

    How pleased have you been with your committee/subcommittee assignments?
        ( ) Pleased   ( ) Neither pleased nor displeased   ( ) Displeased

    Please check if any of the following items characterize your chamber committee system:
        ( ) Most members receive too many committee assignments.
        ( ) Many committees are too large to work effectively.
        ( ) For at least some committees too many proposals are received.
        ( ) For many members the schedule of meetings (committee/subcommittee) creates
            attendance problems.

7. What is the nature of committee staffing in your chamber? (please check)
        ( ) The only staff help committees get is through a central office and generally staff
            members do not attend the committee meetings.
        ( ) Only important committees are assigned specific staff.
        ( ) Most or all committees have at least one staff member assigned.
        ( ) Other _____

    If your committees do receive staff help, which of the following functions do the staff
    members perform?
        ( ) Clerical   ( ) Technical or scientific
        ( ) General information input   ( ) Policy-level advice

8. Do any of the following statements characterize the way committees are managed in your
    chamber? (please check)
        ( ) A committee chairman usually has almost full control over the committee agenda.
        ( ) Most committees are dominated by the chairman.
        ( ) Important committees rely on subcommittee reports.

9. In a typical legislative day, how many hours do you spend on committee work (including meet-
    ings, preparation, information discussion, subcommittee assignments, etc.)? _____
    How many hours do you spend on other work? _____

    Of those hours you spend on committee/subcommittee work, how would you estimate they are
    allocated among the following activities?
    <u># of Hours</u>
        ____ Obtaining information about proposals in order to understand their content.
        ____ Finding out how other committee members feel about the issues (formal and informal
             discussions).
        ____ Hammering out workable compromises with members of the committee(s).
        ____ Reviewing the conduct of administrative agencies.
        ____ Other _____

10. We would now like to turn to your evaluation of specific committees on which you served. Could you name two regular committees on which you served during the most recent session of your legislature? (Please indicate committees that handle legislation. If you served on only one committee of this type, we would appreciate your response regarding it.)

   A. _____   B. _____

   Which of the following items help describe the committee's proceedings during the most recent session? (please check)

Committee A	Committee B	
( )	( )	Held public hearings
( )	( )	Appointed subcommittees
( )	( )	Amended bills in committee
( )	( )	Reviewed conduct of administrative agencies
( )	( )	Amendments were usually made by a voice vote or show of hands rather than a roll call vote
( )	( )	Bills were usually reported out by a voice vote or show of hands rather than a roll call vote

11. It would be very helpful if you could provide the following information for the above two committees:

   Number of staff members assigned? . . . .   A _____ B _____

   Number of meetings per week during last two months of session (estimate)?   A _____ B _____

   If the committee had regular working subcommittees, how many did it have?   A _____ B _____

   Please <u>check</u> if you were chair of either committee . . . .   A _____ B _____

   About how many bills did the committee receive this most recent session?   A _____ B _____

   Which of the two committees (A or B):

		A	B
a.	Has required more of your time	( )	( )
b.	Has seemed more efficient?	( )	( )
c.	Has had a more complex subject matter	( )	( )
d.	Has dealt with more important policies?	( )	( )
e.	Has dealt with issues that cause more disagreement?	( )	( )

   How many members were typically present at a committee meeting? . . . .   A _____ B _____

12. How <u>satisfied</u> were you with those <u>bills that were passed or recommended favorably</u> by the following units of your legislature?

	Degree of Satisfaction					
	very high	high	medium	low	very low	not applicable
Committee A	( )	( )	( )	( )	( )	( )
Committee B	( )	( )	( )	( )	( )	( )
In general, my committees . . . . (if you have more than 2)	( )	( )	( )	( )	( )	( )
The other committees of the chamber	( )	( )	( )	( )	( )	( )
My party caucus	( )	( )	( )	( )	( )	( )
My chamber as a whole	( )	( )	( )	( )	( )	( )

13. How <u>satisfied</u> were you with the decisions <u>not to consider</u>, <u>recommend unfavorably</u>, or defeat bills by the following units?

	very high	high	medium	low	very low	not applicable
Committee A	( )	( )	( )	( )	( )	( )
Committee B	( )	( )	( )	( )	( )	( )
In general, my committees . . . . (if you have more than 2)	( )	( )	( )	( )	( )	( )
The other committees of the chamber . . .	( )	( )	( )	( )	( )	( )
My party caucus	( )	( )	( )	( )	( )	( )
My chamber as a whole	( )	( )	( )	( )	( )	( )

Degree of Satisfaction

14. Apart from the bills, <u>how satisfied</u> were you with <u>the way business was conducted</u> by the following units during the most recent session?

	very high	high	medium	low	very low	not applicable
Committee A	( )	( )	( )	( )	( )	( )
Committee B	( )	( )	( )	( )	( )	( )
In general, my committees . . . . (if you have more than 2)	( )	( )	( )	( )	( )	( )
The other committees of the chamber . . .	( )	( )	( )	( )	( )	( )
My party caucus	( )	( )	( )	( )	( )	( )
My chamber as a whole	( )	( )	( )	( )	( )	( )

Degree of Satisfaction

15. Please indicate if any of the following statements would apply to your experience with Committees A and B during the most recent session:

	Committee A	Committee B
Members of the committee share a similar perspective to a greater degree than do members of my chamber as a whole.	( )	( )
There is often an excessive amount of time consuming debate and discussion before the committee can reach a decision on important issues.	( )	( )
Important committee decisions are often held up because individual legislators are unwilling to compromise.	( )	( )
I usually have a good idea what position my fellow committee members will take on an issue before I discuss it with them.	( )	( )
The committee chairperson usually keeps unnecessary debate and discussion to a minimum.	( )	( )
By the time we understand each others' positions on an issue, there is usually an obvius compromise solution on which committee members can agree.	( )	( )
Most of the debate and discussion is left to subcommittees where most major differences are ironed out.	( )	( )

Bibliography

Agranoff, Robert. 1972. *The New Style in Election Campaigns*. Boston: Holbrook Press.

Black, Duncan. 1958. *The Theory of Committees and Elections*. Cambridge: Cambridge University Press.

Blair, Diane Kincaid, and Ann R. Henry. 1981. "The Family Factor in State Legislative Turnover." *Legislative Studies Quarterly* 6:55–68.

Brams, Steven J. 1975. *Game Theory and Politics*. New York: The Free Press.

Buchanan, James, and Gordon Tullock. 1962. *Calculus of Consent*. Ann Arbor: University of Michigan Press.

Calvert, Jerry. 1979. "Revolving Doors: Volunteerism in State Legislatures." *State Government* 52:174–81.

Chaffey, Douglas C. 1970. "The Institutionalization of State Legislatures: A Comparative Study." *Western Political Quarterly* 23:180–96.

Citizens Conference on State Legislatures. 1971. *The Sometimes Governments*. New York: Bantam.

Clapp, Charles. 1964. *The Congressman: His Work as He Sees It*. Garden City, N.J.: Doubleday-Anchor.

Coombs, Clyde H. 1964. *A Theory of Data*. New York: Wiley.

Cooper, Joseph, and William West. 1981. "The Congressional Career in the 1970s." Chapter in Lawrence C. Dodd and Bruce I. Oppenheimer, *Congress Reconsidered*. Rev. ed. Washington, D.C.: Congressional Quarterly Press.

Council of State Governments. 1980. *The Book of the States, 1980–81*. Lexington, Kentucky.

Dodd, Lawrence C., and Bruce I. Oppenheimer. 1977. *Congress Reconsidered*. New York: Praeger.

Dometrius, Nelson C. 1979. "Measuring Gubernatorial Power." *Journal of Politics* 41:589–610.

Downs, Anthony. 1957. *An Economic Theory of Democracy*. New York: Harper & Row.

Elling, Richard C. 1979. "The Utility of State Legislative Casework as a Means of Oversight." *Legislative Studies Quarterly* 4:353–80.

Eulau, Heinz. 1978. "Changing Views of Representation," in Heinz Eulau and John C. Wahlke, eds., *The Politics of Representation*. Chap. 2. Beverly Hills, Calif.: Sage Publications.

———. 1984. "Legislative Committee Assignments." *Legislative Studies Quarterly* 9:587–634.

Eulau, Heinz, William Buchanan, LeRoy Ferguson, and John Wahlke. 1961. "Career Perspectives of American State Legislators," in Dwaine Marvick, ed. *Political Decision-Makers*. Glencoe: The Free Press. 218–63.

Eulau, Heinz, and Vera McCluggage. 1984. "Standing Committees in Legislatures." *Legislative Studies Quarterly* 9:195–270.

Farquharson, Robin. 1969. *Theory of Voting*. New Haven: Yale University Press.

Fenno, Richard F., Jr. 1962. "The House Appropriations Committee as a Political System." *American Political Science Review* 56:310–24.

———. 1973. *Congressmen in Committees*. Boston: Little, Brown.

Ferejohn, John A. 1974. *Pork Barrel Politics*. Stanford: Stanford University Press.

Fiorina, Morris P. 1977. *Congress: Keystone of the Washington Establishment*. New Haven: Yale University Press.

Fiorina, Morris P., and Charles R. Plott. 1978. "Committee Decisions under Majority Rule." *American Political Science Review* 72:575–98.

Francis, Wayne L. 1967. *Legislative Issues in the Fifty States*. Chicago: Rand McNally.

———. 1962. "Influence and Interaction in a State Legislative Body." *American Political Science Review* 56:953–60.

———. 1982. "Legislative Committee Systems, Optimal Committee Size, and the Cost of Decision Making." *Journal of Politics* 44:822–37.

———. 1985a. "Party Leadership, Party Caucuses, and Committees in the American States." *Legislative Studies Quarterly* 10:243–58.

———. 1985b. "Costs and Benefits of Legislative Service in the American States." *American Journal of Political Science* 29:626–42.

Francis, Wayne L., and James W. Riddlesperger. 1982. "U.S. State Legislative Committees: Structure, Procedural Efficiency, and Party Control." *Legislative Studies Quarterly* 7:453–71.

Francis, Wayne L., and John R. Baker. 1986. "Why Do U.S. State Legislators Vacate Their Seats." *Legislative Studies Quarterly* 11:119–26.

Friedrich, Robert J. 1982. "In Defense of Multiplicative Terms in Multiple Regression Equations." *American Journal of Political Science* 26:797–833.

Goldfeld, S. M., and R. E. Quandt. 1965. "Some Tests for Heteroskedasticity." *Journal of the American Statistical Association* 60:539–47.

Hain, Paul L. 1974. "Age, Ambitions, and Political Careers: The Middle-Age Crisis." *Western Political Quarterly* 27:265–74.

Hamm, Keith E. 1980. "U.S. State Legislative Committee Decisions: Similar Results in Different Settings." *Legislative Studies Quarterly* 5:31–54.

———. 1982. "Consistency Between Committee and Floor Voting in U.S. State Legislatures." *Legislative Studies Quarterly* 7:473–90.

Hamm, Keith E., Robert Harmel, and Robert Thompson. 1983. "Ethnic and Partisan Minorities in Two Southern State Legislatures." *Legislative Studies Quarterly* 8:177–90.

Hamm, Keith E., and Roby Robertson. 1981. "Factors Influencing the Adoption of New Methods of Legislative Oversight in the U.S. States." *Legislative Studies Quarterly* 6:133–50.

Hedlund, Ronald D. 1984. "Organizational Attributes of Legislatures: Structure, Rules, Norms, Resources." *Legislative Studies Quarterly* 9:51–121.

Hedlund, Ronald D., and Patricia K. Freeman. 1981. "A Strategy for Measuring the Performance of Legislatures in Processing Decisions." *Legislative Studies Quarterly* 6:87–113.

Hedlund, Ronald D., and Keith Hamm. 1978. "Institutional Innovation and Performance Effectiveness in Public Policy Making," in Leroy N. Rieselbach, ed., *Legislative Reform: The Policy Impact*. Lexington, Mass.: Lexington Books: 117–32.

Hibbing, John R. 1982. "Voluntary Retirement from the U.S. House: The Costs of Congressional Service." *Legislative Studies Quarterly* 7:57–73.

Huitt, Ralph K. 1954. "The Congressional Committee: A Case Study." *American Political Science Review* 48:340–65.

———. 1961. "Democratic Party Leadership in the Senate." *American Political Science Review* 55:331–44.

Hyneman, Charles S. 1938. "Tenure and Turnover of Legislative Personnel." *Annals of the American Academy of Political and Social Science* 195:21–31.

Jacoby, William G., and Wayne L. Francis. 1985. "Scaling Legislative Decision-Making: A Methodological Exercise." *Political Behavior* 7:285–303.

Jewell, Malcolm E. 1982. *Representation in State Legislatures*. Lexington, Ky.: University of Kentucky Press.

Jewell, Malcolm E., and Samuel C. Patterson. 1973. *The Legislative Process in the United States*. New York: Random House.

Kingdon, John W. 1977. "Models of Legislative Voting." *Journal of Politics* 39:563–95.

Kostroski, Warren L. 1977. "Elections and Legislative Reform: External and Internal Influences on Legislative Behavior." *Policy Studies Journal* 5 (Summer):414–18.

Lees, John D., and Malcolm Shaw, eds. 1979. *Committees in Legislatures: A Comparative Analysis*. Durham, N.C.: Duke University Press.

Liebowitz, Arleen, and Robert Tollison. 1980. "A Theory of Legislative Organization: Making the Most of Your Majority." *Quarterly Journal of Economics* 94:261–77.

Lowi, Theodore J. 1964. "American Business, Public Policy, Case-Studies, and Political Theory." *World Politics* 16:677–715.

Manley, John. 1965. "The House Committee on Ways and Means: Conflict Management in a Congressional Committee." *American Political Science Review* 59:927–39.

Matthews, Donald R. 1959. "The Folkways of the United States Senate: Conformity to Group Norms and Legislative Effectiveness." *American Political Science Review* 53:1064–1089.

———. 1960. *U.S. Senators and Their World*. Chapel Hill, N.C.: University of North Carolina Press.

Mayhew, David R. 1974. *Congress: The Electoral Connection*. New Haven: Yale University Press.

McConachie, Lauros G. 1898. *Congressional Committees*. New York: Crowell.

Mezey, Michael L. 1979. *Comparative Legislatures*. Durham, N.C.: Duke University Press.

Murphy, James T. 1974. "Political Parties and the Pork Barrel: Party Conflict and Cooperation in House Public Works Committee Decision Making." *American Political Science Review* 68:169–85.

Olson, David M. 1980. *The Legislative Process: A Comparative Approach*. New York: Harper & Row.

Ornstein, Norman J., Thomas E. Mann, Michael Malbin, Allen Schick, and John F. Bibby. 1984. *Vital Statistics on Congress, 1984–85*. Washington, D.C.: American Enterprise Institute.

Parker, Glenn R. 1986. *Homeward Bound: Exploring Changes in Congressional Behavior*. Pittsburgh: University of Pittsburgh Press.

Pitkin, Hanna F. 1967. *The Concept of Representation.* Berkeley and Los Angeles: University of California Press.

Polsby, Nelson W. 1968. "The Institutionalization of the U.S. House of Representatives." *American Political Science Review* 62:144–68.

Rae, Douglas W. 1969. "Decision Rules and Individual Values in Constitutional Choice." *American Political Science Review* 68:40–56.

Ray, Bruce A., and Steven S. Smith. 1984. "Committee Size in the U.S. Congress." *Legislative Studies Quarterly* 9:679–95.

Ray, David R. 1974. "Membership Stability in Three State Legislatures: 1893–1969." *American Political Science Review* 68:106–112.

Riker, William H., and Peter C. Ordeshook. 1973. *An Introduction to Positive Political Theory.* Englewood Cliffs, N.J.: Prentice-Hall.

Ripley, Randall B., and Grace A. Franklin. 1984. *Congress, the Bureaucracy, and Public Policy.* Homewood, Il.: Dorsey Press.

Rohde, David W. 1979. "Risk-bearing and Progressive Ambition: The Case of the United States House of Representatives." *American Journal of Political Science* 23:1–26.

Rohde, David W., and Kenneth A. Shepsle. 1973. "Democratic Committee Assignments in the House of Representatives: Some Aspects of Strategic Choice." *American Political Science Review* 67:889–905.

Rosenthal, Alan. 1974a. *Legislative Performance in the States.* New York: The Free Press.

———. 1974b. "Turnover in State Legislatures." *American Journal of Political Science* 18:609–16.

Rosenthal, Alan, and Rod Forth. 1978. "The Assembly Line: Law Production in the American States." *Legislative Studies Quarterly* 3:265–92.

Schlesinger, Joseph. 1965. "The Politics of the Executive," in Herbert Jacob and Kenneth N. Vines, eds., *Politics in the American States.* Boston: Little, Brown & Co.; 207–38.

Shepsle, Kenneth A. 1978. *The Giant Jigsaw Puzzle: Democratic Committee Assignments in the Modern House.* Chicago: University of Chicago Press.

———. 1979. "Institutional Arrangements and Equilibrium in Multidimensional Voting Models." *American Journal of Political Science* 23:27–59.

Shepsle, Kenneth A., and Barry R. Weingast. 1981. "Political Preferences for the Pork Barrel: A Generalization." *American Journal of Political Science* 25:96–111.

Simon, Herbert A. 1957. *Models of Man.* New York: Wiley.

Torgerson, Warren. 1958. *Theory and Methods of Scaling.* New York: Wiley.

Uslaner, Eric M., and Ronald E. Weber. 1977. *Patterns of Decision-Making in State Legislatures.* New York: Praeger.

Wahlke, John C. 1978. "Policy Demands and System Support: The Role of the Representative," in Heinz Eulau and John C. Wahlke, eds., *The Politics of Representation.* Chap. 4. Beverly Hills, Calif.: Sage Publications.

Wahlke, John C., Heinz Eulau, William Buchanan, and LeRoy C. Ferguson. 1962. *The Legislative System: Explorations in Legislative Behavior.* New York: Wiley.

Weingast, Barry R. 1979. "A Rational Choice Perspective on Congressional Norms." *American Journal of Political Science* 23:245–63.

Westefield, Louis P. 1974. "Majority Party Leadership and the Committee System in the House of Representatives." *American Political Science Review* 68:1593–604.

Wiggins, Charles W., and E. Lee Bernick. 1977. "Legislative Turnover Reconsidered." *Policy Studies Journal* 3 (Summer): 419–24.

Wilson, Woodrow. 1885. *Congressional Government.* Boston: Houghton Mifflin.

Winslow, C. I. 1931. *State Legislative Committees: A Study in Procedure.* Baltimore: Johns Hopkins University Press.

Index

Accommodation in committee assignments, 26, 29, 50, 143–44, 146–50
Action, demands for, 9, 103, 123, 143
Adaptation: structural and behavioral, 116–19
Age: and turnover, 84, 86, 88, 89, *table* 91
Agendas, 2, 73, 116, 143; of individual legislators, 20–21, 22–25, 52–53, 145–46; and party leadership, 20–22, 38, 73, 143; setting of, 17–19, 22–36, 39, 52–53
Alaska senate, 59
Amendments, 14, 18–19, 33, 123n
Appropriations, 34–35, 144
Appropriations committee, 34, 51
Arkansas legislature, 85
Authority, delegation of, 97
Authorization committees, 34
Autonomous committees, 125–26
Autonomous individual actions, 98

Bargaining, 6–7, 98, 107, 126, 136
Benefits of legislative decision making, 70, 73–74, 124–25, 151
Bernick, E. Lee, 84
Bicameral systems, 33
Biennial session, 72
Bills, 14, 16, 23, 70, 123; assignments in Indiana legislature, 150; drafting services, 53; and legislator satisfaction, 80; passage rate, 53–65, 73–82, 149; sponsorship, 23–25, 53, 65, 89, 145–49
Binary voting, 14, 15
Bipartisan decision making, 40–41
Black, Duncan, 1
Blair, Diane Kincaid, 84, 85, 87, 90
Buchanan, James, 100–102, 106, 108
Budgets, 34, 144–45

Calculus of Consent, The (Buchanan and Tullock), 100–102
California legislature, 25, 150
Calvert, Jerry, 85
Career, legislative, 4–5, 92–93
Career, outside: maintenance by legislators, 71
Career ambitions and legislator turnover, 84, 86, 88–89, 90, *table* 91
Carter, Jimmy, 52, 145
Casework, 73, 83
Caucus. *See* Party caucus
Centralization of decision making, 47, 49, 52–53, 58–60, 63, 65
Chaffey, Douglas C., 5
Chairs. *See* Committee chairs; Subcommittee chairs
Chambers, 2, 19, 61, 78, 98–99; size, 45–46, 114–21
Chief executive: as legislator's vote model, 125, 126; role in agenda setting, 52, 143
Citizens Conference on State Legislatures, 80, 152
Closed-input system of proposals, 123n
Coalition favoritism and committee chair positions, 50–51
Collective choice as source of complexity, 126–29
Committee assignments, 21, 25–32, 36, 40, 93; accommodation in, 26–29, 50, 143–44, 146–50; in joint committees, 120; as means of party leader control, 38, 41
Committee chairs, 36, 49–51, 88–89, 93, 109; and agendas, 40, 143; appointments to, 21, 36, 143–44, 147; bill passage rate, 61, 63, 65, 148; and party leadership, 37–39
Committee size, 50, 107–8, 136; and

Committee size (*continued*)
  assignment accommodation, 28–31,
  147; and attendance rates, 117–18;
  and chamber size, 45–46, 116; of
  joint committees, 120; optimal, 103,
  106, 109, 115, 121, 133
Committee of the Whole, 19
Committees: appointment of, 136, 150;
  approval of member-sponsored bills,
  147; attendance, 61–62, 117–18,
  120; and decision making, 38,
  41–46, 58–59, 99; definition of,
  1–2; jurisdictions, 13–14, 32–36;
  satisfaction with outcomes of, 47–50;
  structure, 8–9, 97, 104; system
  types, 53, 119–21, 131–39; theoretical model for, 107–9; work distributions, *table* 103. *See also*
  Appropriations committee; Autonomous committees; Committee of
  the Whole; Interim committees;
  Semiautonomous committees;
  Subcommittees
Communities of interest: as factor in decision making, 49, 51
Complexity: due to collective nature of
  choice, 124, 126–29; of preferences,
  129–34; use of committee system to
  minimize, 131–39
Compromise, 65, 126
Conference committee action, 145
Congress, U.S., 4–5, 37, 65, 71, 90;
  agenda setting, 18–19, 53; appropriations and authorization, 34; bill passage rate, 64; committee assignment
  process, 25–26, 27; influence on
  state legislature practices, 152; om-
  nibus bill as example of inseparable
  preferences, 16; standing committees,
  3, 6–7; turnover in, 83
"Congressional Committee, The: A
  Case Study" (Huitt), 3
Congressional Committees (Mc-
  Conachie), 3
Congressional Government (Wilson), 3
Congressional Quarterly study on legis-
  lator pay and sessions, 72–73
Connecticut legislature, 83, 120
Constituency makeup and committee as-
  signments, 26, 27
Constituency service, 65
Constituents: and open-input system, 122
Cost-benefit perspective analysis, 70–82

Costs: as work put into sponsored legislation, 70–73. *See also* Decision
  costs; External costs; Opportunity
  costs; Private decision costs
Cyclical majorities: role in amendment
  process, 19

Decentralization of decision making,
  22–36, 52–53, 58–60, 63–64
Decision costs, 70–73, 106, 109, 124;
  reduction of, 99–102, 104, 116; in
  theoretical model, 107–9
Decision making, 6–7, 58–60,
  97–105, 123; bargaining as instrument of, 6–7, 98, 107; benefits of,
  70, 73–74, 124–25, 151; centralization, 47, 49, 58–60, 63, 65; complexity, 129–39, 150; costs of. *See*
  Decision costs; External costs; decentralization, 22–36, 52–53,
  58–60, 63–64; delegation of, 7, 40,
  97–100; risks, 98–99, 102, 104
Deficit financing as restriction on legislation, 145
Delay as decision delegation tactic, 98
Discipline and party leadership, 37–38,
  61
Distributive decisions, 21
Distributive Legislative Game, 144
Distributive policies and omnibus legis-
  lation, 144
Dometrius, Nelson C., 52
Downs, Anthony, 8
Duplication in bicameral systems, 33

Executive, the, 152
Executive agencies and corresponding
  committees, 32
Executive committee, 2
Executive functions and corresponding
  committees, 32
Expense allowances: emphasis on in
  Congress, 83
Experience and committee assignments,
  26
Expertise and legislative information, 8,
  84
External (whole life) circumstances as
  influence on legislators, 150–51
External costs, 106, 109, 124; in open-
  input system, 123–24; reduction of,
  116; in theoretical model, 107–9

Face-to-face groups, 1, 7
Factionalism and bill passage rates, 61–63
Family needs: as legislator's opportunity costs, 151; and legislator turnover, 84, 86–87, *table* 91
Fenno, Richard F., Jr., 3
Ferejohn, John A., 18–19
Fiscal matters, committees on, 34
Floor, the: as decision-making locus, 41, 58–59, 126; as personal agenda hurdle, 145
Floor fight as continuation of committee disagreement, 36
Force as instrument of decision making, 6, 98
Formal hearing as legislative hurdle, 19
Freeman, Patricia K., 74

Game theory and complexity of human preference, 13
Goldfeld, S. M., 75, 79
Good will as means of party leader control, 38
Governor, 52, 58–59, 73; and the item veto, 144–45; as legislative decision maker, 41, 43; as legislator's vote model, 125, 126

Hain, Paul L., 84, 88
Hamm, Keith E., 41
Health and legislator turnover, 86, 89, *table* 91
Hedlund, Ronald D., 74
Henry, Ann R., 84, 85, 87, 90
Heteroskedasticity, test for, 75, 79
Higher office: as reason for leaving legislature, 86. *See also* Career ambitions and legislator turnover
Huitt, Ralph, 3
Hyneman, Charles S., 85

Incentive structure and legislator turnover, 84
Index to House and Senate Journals (Indiana): bills sent to ways and means committee, 34–35
Indiana legislature, 34–35, 150; bill sponsorship, 23–24, 27–32; legislator turnover, 85–92
Indifference curves and opportunity cost of legislators, 81–82

Indifference relationships and saliency of preferences, 127n
Industrial states: chamber size and decision making, 43
Information, 16–17, 65; as instrument of decision making, 6–8, 98
Inseparable preferences, 15–16, 18–19, 33, 53, 134; and outcome preference sets, 128; and use of subcommittees, 137–39, 145
Interdependence in legislative committees, 2
Interest groups, 5, 143
Interest-advocacy accommodation syndrome, 25–26
Interim committees, 70, 80
Internal sponsorship of committee bills, 29, 32
Interpersonal behavior, 116–19, 137–38
Interpersonal complexities and majority voting, 126
Interpersonal decision costs, 101, 109
Interpersonal time costs, 102
Iowa legislature, 135
Item veto: governors' use of, 144–45

Jewell, Malcolm E., 71
Joint committees, 34, 119–21
Jurisdictions, 44, 53; as constraint on committees, 13–14; overlapping of, 2; of standing committees, 32–36

Labor, division of, 4, 99–100
Legislation: and bill passage rate, 53–65, 73–82, 149; increase in as trend, 151; processing of, 143, 150–51; volume of, 63, 124–26
Legislative compensation, 70–73, 82, 85
Legislative dissatisfaction and legislator turnover, 86–88, 89–90, *table* 91
Legislative histories and basic trends, 151–52
Legislative incentive system and reelection possibilities, 92–93
Legislative oversight of administrative agencies, 65
Legislative session, length of, 78, 125, 126, 151
Legislatures, 1–6; part-time status of, 80
Liebowitz, Arleen, 20–21, 22, 38

Likert-type scale, use of, 47, 87
Lobbyists, 8, 28, 99
Logrolling, 18, 36
Lower chambers and use of subcommittees, 135
Lowi, Theodore J., 21, 144

McCluggage, Vera, 3
McConachie, Lauros, 3
Maine legislature, 120
Majority party: bill passage rate of, 61–63, 74–80; and committee assignments, 26; leaders as significant decision makers, 41–46, 58–59
Majority voting, 14; as source of complexity, 126–29
Management by committee, 20, 21
Massachusetts legislature, 70, 120
Maximum preference complexity, 129–30, 132
Mean satisfaction rating, 75
Media outlets and information reports, 8
Memory, procedural: and legislator turnover, 84
Michigan legislature, 83
Minimum preference complexity, 129–30, 131–32
Minor bills, 80
Minority party, 75; and bill passage rate, 61, 74; caucus decision satisfaction, 49–50; and committee assignments, 26, 40; and voluntary retirees, 85–86n
Missouri legislature: bill sponsorship in, 23–24, 27–32; legislator turnover, 85–92
Multiple centers of legislative decisions, 45
Mutual accommodation, 22n

Nebraska legislature, 74
New Hampshire senate, 77–78, 80
New York legislature, 25
Newspaper polls, 99
Nonzero-sum game, 28

Oklahoma senate, 59
Omnibus legislation, 16, 80, 144–45
One-party dominance and decision making, 42
Open-input system of proposals, 122–24

Opportunity costs, 80, 82, 150–51; in nonpublic sector, 69, 71; as reason for legislator turnover, 86–87, 89–90, *table* 91
Optimality: of committee size, 103, 106, 109, 115, 121, 133; of committee system, 106, 121
Ordeshook, Peter C., 19
Ordinary least squares (OLS), 75
Organizational efficiency and personal agenda items, 145
Ornstein, Norman J., 64
Over-accommodation in committee game playing, 150
Oversight: importance in state legislatures, 73
Overtime and legislator benefits, 151

Partisanship, 40–41
Part-time legislatures, 69–70, 80
Party caucus, 3, 41–51, 99; as decision-making locus, 58–59; as personal agenda hurdle, 145
Party leadership, 26, 41–46, 99, 144; and agendas, 20–22, 38, 73, 143; and committee assignments, 26; and committee leadership, 37–39, 43
Passage rate of bills, 53–65, 73–82, 149
Patronage and committee expansion, 105
Pay. *See* Salary (Pay), legislative
Per diem, 82, 85, 151
Personal background and committee assignments, 26, 27
Policy committee as source of decisions, 41
Political factors in legislator turnover, 84
Political preferences and chair appointments, 143–44
Poll as decision-making factor, 99, 104
Polsby, Nelson, 4
Preference maps, 14–16
Preferences, individual, 6–8, 13–19, 97, 149; and chair appointments, 143–44; complexity, 129–34; to defeat, 14, 15–16, 47–48, 126–29; to pass, 14, 15–16, 47–48, 129–29; patterns, 126–29. *See also* Inseparable preferences; Separable preferences
Pre-legislative session: and decision making, 42

President, U.S., 52, 145
Presiding officers as decision makers, 41–46, 58–59
Private decision costs, 101, 102, 109
Private employment, 81–82, 151
Private status: as viewed by congressmen and state legislators, 90–91
Procedural problems and bill passage rates, 61–63
Proposals, legislative, 14, 17–19, 36, 112–24, 134

Quality control in open-input system, 123
Quality of membership and legislator turnover, 84
Quandt, R. E., 75–79

Rank-and-file legislators, agendas of, 20, 22–25, 143
Ray, David R., 83–84
Reciprocity, 28, 29, 36, 38, 51; and agenda setting, 53, 145; to defeat legislation, 34; and sponsorship success, 147; as stabilization norm, 21–22, 22n; vote-favors as, 17
Reelection, 6, 83, 91–92
Representation through use of open-input system, 122–24
Representatives, U.S. House of, 3–6
Responsibilities, delegation of, 6–7, 98
Retirement age, 86, 89, *table* 91
Revenues: as appropriation restrictions, 145; use of referendum for, 98
Review, multiple: as means of managing decision risks, 99
Riker, William H., 19
Risk: and decision making, 98–99, 102, 104; and volume of legislation, 124
Risk of defeat and size of standing committee, 116
Rohde, David W., 90, 92
Rosenthal, Alan, 4
Rules, legislature, 104–5, 136
Rural states: chamber sizes and decision making, 43

Salary (Pay), legislative, 72–73, 81–82, 85; and session length, 151
Saliency of preference, 14–16, 127–28, 146–47
Satisfaction ratings: and bill passage

rates, 73–82; between party caucuses and committees, 47–50
Scheduling: and bill passage rate, 61–62, 63, 65, 148
Schlesinger, Joseph, 52
Seat distribution, 46
Self-interest and legislator turnover, 83–93
Semiautonomous committees, 125–26
Senate chambers: use of subcommittees, 135
Seniority: in Congress, 4, 37; in state legislatures, 26, 143–44
Separable preferences, 14–16, 18, 33–36, 127–29, 134
Session length, 70, 78, 80; and cost-benefit analysis, 71–73
Sessions, biennial, 72
Shepsle, Kenneth A., 6, 25–26, 27
Simons, Herbert A., 8
Sometime Governments, The (Citizens Conference on State Legislatures), 80, 152
South Carolina legislature, 23
Special sessions, 70, 85, 151
Sponsorship, 24, 53, 65, 89, 145–49; increases in, 125, 126, 151–52
Staff, 8; increases in, 125, 126, 151–52
Structuralism: and decision making, 45, 116–19; and sponsorship success, 65
Subcommittee chairs, 40, 143–44
Subcommittees, 1–3, 4, 135–39; and agenda setting, 39–40, 53; and appropriation process, 34; autonomous and semiautonomous, 125–26; Congressional, 64, 83; and decision costs, 109, 113–14; and decision making, 42, 58–59, 126; and inseparable preferences, 137–39; jurisdictional restraints on, 13–14; legislative processing, 19, 143; use of, 5, 114–17, 144, 151
Subject-matter designations, 33
Successive voting procedure, 14

Tax matters, use of referendums for, 98
Texas legislature, 23, 150
Theory of Committees and Elections, The (Black), 1
Time constraints on committees, 13–14
Time costs: of information on members' positions, 136; of legislative decision making, 70–73, 77

Time demands of legislators, 103
Tollison, Robert, 20–21, 22, 38
Tullock, Gordon, 100–102, 106, 108
Turnover of legislators, 83–93

Universal Legislative Game, 144–45
Unrelated bills and separable prefer-
     ences, 16
Utah legislature, 135

Veto, 51, 126, 144–45
Voluntary self-selected committee,
     97–98
Vote trading, 6–7, 17, 18, 33
Voting, 14; changing of by legislators,
     16–17, 41; as means of committee
     decision, 97–98; as source of com-
     plexity, 126–29
Voting, sophisticated, 17; and separable
     preferences, 33, 36

Ways and means committee, 34–35, 51
Weighted least squares (WLS), 75
Weingast, Barry R., 21–22, 144
Whole life (external) circumstances: as
     influence on legislators, 150–51
Wiggins, Charles W., 84
Wilson, Woodrow, 3
Wins, 22, 28, 73
Winslow, C. I., 3
Wisconsin legislature, 83
Work distribution in legislative day,
     table 103
Workdays, legislative, 69–73, 82, 85;
     and bill passage success, 151; in-
     crease of to meet action demands,
     103–4; and majority party satisfac-
     tion, 74–80; and opportunity costs,
     80; and private occupation income,
     86; and reelection bids, 92
Workload of individual legislator, 100

Zero-sum game, 21, 144